UPPER MISSISSIPPI VALLEY BY MOTORCYCLE

By Kay Fellows

The Motorcycle Publishing Company
An Imprint of Far Horizons Media Company

(Formerly Motorcycling, an Imprint of Bristol Fashion Publishing Company)

Far Horizons Media Company is a Division of NetPV, Inc.

Published by
The Motorcycle Publishing Company
www.MotorcyclePublishing.com

An Imprint of Far Horizons Media Company
www.FarHorizonsMedia.com

(Formerly Motorcycling, an Imprint of Bristol Fashion Publishing Company)

Far Horizons Media Company is a Division of NetPV, Inc.
www.NetPV.com

ISBN: 1-892216-56-6

LCCN: 2006-922352

2

DEDICATION

For

Lynne, Wendell, & Hal

Thanks to

Danny Anderson
Diane Solis
Laurie Foltz
Kay Folsom
Matt & Ellen Littrel
Garth Littrel
Pat James
Laurie Daniel
Paul Rucker
Wendell Cook
Harold Cook
Jon Pyse
Steve & Nancy Pomeroy
Howard Brady
Will and Susan Standley
All the bikers who agreed to pose for pictures
The Wednesday Morning Writer's Group
My online buddies
All the helpful and friendly people up and down the river
And most especially to
Lynne Howe
Jody Nelson
Jeff Alls
Steve Burns

CONTENTS

INTRODUCTION

Legend has it that as The Great Father of Waters pushed his way through the middle of the land heading toward the oceans, he encountered an area so beautiful that he turned his head for a second look. This caused him to veer off course. The Illinois/Iowa Quad Cities (Davenport, Bettendorf, Rock Island, and Moline) mark the only place where the Mississippi River flows east to west.

Geologists have a less colorful explanation for the area. A map of North America depicting the last Ice Age shows a thin streak of green cutting into the otherwise white surface. Almost in the dead center, this green strip shows where the glacier had a break in its surface. Here the tremendous force that flattened the land for hundreds of miles to the East and West pushed up a narrow band of rocky limestone and sandstone cliffs. This area, approximately twenty-five miles wide and three hundred fifty miles long, formed the Upper Mississippi Valley.

A paradise for motorcyclists, the valley follows the Mississippi River from roughly the Quad Cities north to the twin cities of Minneapolis and St. Paul. Between these two points are scenic bluffs with spectacular overlooks of the river, winding roads cutting through the hills, historic river towns, restored villages, open air markets, ethnic communities, and some of the finest Wisconsin cheese available anywhere.

The Great River Road traverses the east and west sides of the Mississippi, and includes both main highways and many excellent side roads. On the east side of the river the area is quite wide, with the hills and bluffs stretching halfway across Illinois and Wisconsin. The band is narrower to the west side in Minnesota and Iowa, but the scenery is equally spectacular.

Easy access to the dams spaced along the length of the river is provided. Here you can take a break and watch an array of barges and pleasure boats lock through.

Bridges over the river allow bikers to make short day loops or to spend a week or more exploring all the sights and side trips. Several smaller rivers flow into the Mississippi and offer many opportunities for exploration.

Accommodations run the gamut from primitive campgrounds, well-maintained state parks, or private facilities, to quaint hotels and motels to provide a good night's rest. Throughout the valley fine dining awaits at almost every stop.

During the year, many of the towns have celebrations honoring their histories. For example, the residents of Fulton, Illinois, wear wooden shoes and wash the main street during Dutch Days. Festivals recognize the contributions of everything from riverboats and bald eagles to watermelons and mallards.

The area is especially rewarding in the fall, as riders enjoy taking the fantastic color tours. Many motorcycle clubs plan all year for this event, but for those who like to explore in smaller groups or on their own, the possibilities are endless. As an added bonus, the day is often finished with a breathtaking sunset.

The Upper Mississippi River National Wildlife Refuge extends 261 miles from Rock Island, Illinois, to Wabasha, Minnesota. Encompassing 200,000 acres of water, wooded islands, marshes, forest, and prairie, the refuge sports 292 species of birds, 57 species of mammals, 118 species of fish, and some 45 species of amphibians and reptiles. For some this is their permanent home; others are just temporary residents. The refuge is a major flyway for migrating birds and a wintering ground for bald eagles. Over three million visitors a year make this the most heavily-used National Wildlife Refuge in the country.

In this guidebook I focus on the interesting and scenic back roads and less-publicized attractions. The more famous sites along the way are well documented and easily discovered, so I won't be covering them in great detail.

Some of the roads listed will provide exhilarating and challenging rides. It goes without saying that you must be alert and watchful while traveling these byways.

Now that we know a bit about the area, it's time to rev up those engines and explore the most beautiful countryside that the Midwest has to offer.

Kay Fellows

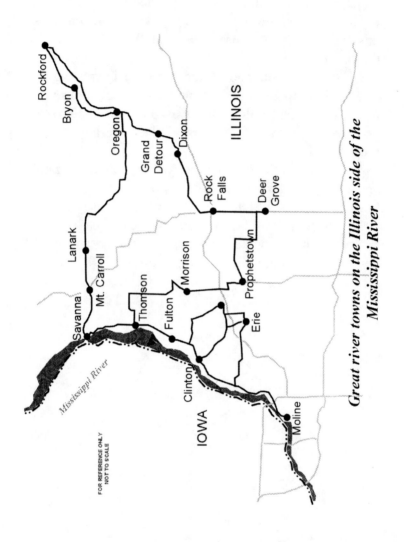

Great river towns on the Illinois side of the Mississippi River

CHAPTER ONE

THE RIVER TOWNS

River road Route 84 leads north from Moline on the Illinois side of the Mississippi. This stretch of highway links great little towns: Hampton, Rapids City, Port Byron, Cordova, Albany, Fulton, Thomson, and up to Savanna, all with sights worth seeing. Other towns, on side roads fun to ride, are popular destinations. A couple of days of touring and stopping will give bikers an intimate view of this section of upper Mississippi country.

From the small park on Campbell's Island it is easy to see the bend in the river. The island, at the northeastern edge of the Quad Cities, is a good place to relax and plan your trip. The monument in the park is for soldiers and settlers killed in the Black Hawk War. In contrast, there is also a Peace Garden honoring the Sauk and Mesquakie (Fox) tribes who inhabited the area in the early 1800s.

Heading upriver on Highway 84, you'll arrive at Hampton. Here at the Heritage Center are ever-changing displays and exhibits showing the history of the valley. You won't want to miss the fantastic Ginkgo tree. This piece of historical art is carved to depict those living along the river. Human, animal, and plant life all are represented. If the center is closed it is still possible to see the tree through the windows.

Black's store, a small museum devoted to history displays of the area, is also in Hampton and is open on weekend afternoons during the summer.

Mosaic representations of Native American beadwork decorate the circular Peace Garden on Campbell's Island.

Rapids City boasts the Brother's Family Restaurant, a favorite stop for bikers looking for a fine meal.

You also can relax at the riverfront in Rapids City and be soothed by the flowing water, or you can continue a few miles farther up 84 and do your relaxing in the waterfront park in Port Byron.

Illiniwek County Forest Preserve features riverside camping. There's also a nature spiral consisting of several small boulders, many decorated with animal or plant drawings. Those wishing to stretch their legs a bit can cross Route 84 and climb to the scenic overlook for a great view of the river.

Each year in mid-August the town of Port Byron is filled to overflowing, for it is the Illinois site for the Great River Tug Fest. This weekend event pits teams from Illinois and Iowa against each other in a tug of war across the Mississippi River. The rivalry is strong as the teams vie for bragging rights for the coming year.

Continuing up Route 84, you can make a fuel stop at either of two stations along the highway or grab a meal at Scenic Road Restaurant. If you like, you also can make a turn east on Cordova Road which will provide some nice sweepers as you head over to Erie, or you can remain heading north along the river.

An Indian warrior, an eagle, and a white settler are only some of the carvings on the Ginkgo tree at the Hampton Heritage Center.

If you enjoy watching the fast-paced sport of drag racing, you will enjoy a visit to the Cordova Dragstrip. During the last weekend in August, the dragstrip hosts the World Series of Drag Racing; other top-flight events are held on weekends during the summer.

North on 84 is the village of Albany, about twenty-five miles from Moline. Here you may browse through several antique shops or eat a meal and plan your itinerary at one of two fine restaurants. The intimate atmosphere of the Mississippi Cafe is quite cozy, or perhaps you'd prefer Julie's Cafe where you can sit at the big picture window overlooking the river and watch barges and eagles. If it's evening, Ammon's Landing is a favorite of motorcyclists and has easy access for those arriving by boat.

North of Albany, you travel about six miles to cross Route 30 at Fulton. Following the Mississippi north on highway 84 makes for a scenic ride toward Wisconsin. The many bridges over the river allow bikers to make short day loops or spend a week or more exploring all the sights and side trips that enrich the area.

As an alternate route out of Albany, swing toward the southeast on Albany Road. Just at the top of the bluff is the entrance to Albany Mounds State Preserve. Here in prehistoric times the Middle Woodland people constructed several burial mounds above the town. Artifacts discovered by archeologists at the site of the nearby village show that this was an active trade center. Shells from the Gulf of Mexico, obsidian from Wyoming, and copper from the Upper Great Lakes all have been found at Albany Mounds.

A few miles farther east on Albany Road, you can turn off on Diamond Road for a trip back over to the river. There are a couple of nice sweepers on this road. Or you can continue for thirteen miles to the town of Erie, which is a popular stopping spot for poker runs. Often, on weekends, the triangle park in the center of town is lined with motorcycles, while bikers visit the

Glass Rail, The Other Place, or the Depot, all located on the "three-sided square." Breakfast can be found at Russ' Café on the triangle, or you can stop at the Erie Greens Restaurant located at Lake Erie Country Club. The Greens is open daily from 6:00 a.m. until 9:00 p.m. For fast food you can choose either the Pink Pony or PJ's restaurant.

A mile out of Erie on Moline Road, turn on Wilmot Road. Follow Wilmot to the stop sign and then turn right onto Burns Road, to the village of Fenton. A stop at Payne's Grocery allows you to enter an authentic old-fashioned small town store. Lena Payne has operated the store with almost no changes for over fifty years. You can sit on the worn old bench where the problems of the world have been discussed and solved by the local residents for half a century and enjoy a cool soda while visiting a piece of our fast-disappearing past.

Payne's Grocery in Fenton is a place to stop and unwind from the hectic pace of modern life. Taking a break here are Paul Rucker, Garth Littrel, Pat James, Matt Littrel, and Ellen Littrel.

An easy ride along the bottom of the hills on the Fenton blacktop takes you up to the Garden Plain Road and a left turn that brings you back to Highway 84. Both soft serve and hand-dipped ice cream, along with sandwiches and appetizers, can be found at KaM's Drive Inn sitting beside the highway a couple of miles north of Albany.

For anyone interested in Native American culture and history, I suggest a visit to the Bear Land Trading Post, a mile south of Route 30. Trade goods, Indian artifacts, southwestern décor, and a Native American museum all can be found at this one site.

Sitting just north of Route 30, the small town of Fulton, Illinois, takes great pride in its Dutch heritage. The shoreline of the river is dominated by the large windmill which was fabricated in and imported from the Netherlands. Dutch craftsmen came over and erected the windmill on a flood control dike. It serves not only as the focal point of the community, but the base also houses a visitors' welcome and information center and a gift shop.

Winding around behind the mill is a walkway to the top of the dike where you can take a leisurely river stroll and watch the boats and barges dotting the water or enjoy a picnic lunch in the adjacent park.

The first weekend in May is set aside for the annual Dutch Days Festival. Colorful tulips are in bloom all over the town, and many of the citizens don authentic Dutch clothing including wooden shoes. Traditional activities include Dutch dancing, a Dutch costume fashion show, street scrubbing, and many other activities. Saturday afternoon is highlighted by a large parade down the freshly-scrubbed street. The village is home to several unique shops. The newest business is the Fulton Fiber Mill, which uses computerized machines to spin yarn from the coats of sheep, alpacas, llamas, and even longhaired dogs. They produce rovings and batts for

hand-spinners and yarn for do-it-yourselfers. The gift
shop next door offers an assortment of finished fiber
goods.

*Dominating the Riverfront in Fulton is "De Immigrant," a windmill
fabricated in the Netherlands and erected on the flood control dike.*

Other shops of interest to the traveler include
Artistry in Gifts and Glass, which features fine jewelry,
gifts, mosaic tables, and artwork made of stained glass.
Susan's Calico Creations specializes in quilts and
quilting fabric, notions, and patterns.

Wildlife preservation is the focus of Wildwood
Farms, which manufactures redwood bird and squirrel
feeders, bird houses, and similar products.

Don't miss a visit to Heritage Canyon, a restored
settlement from the mid-1800s inside an old twelve-acre
quarry. Winding paths take you through the village and
up the bluffs to a small farmstead. A swinging bridge, a
covered bridge, and a waterfall add a splash of interest to
your visit.

Citizens of all ages participate in the street scrubbing during the annual Dutch Days Festival in Fulton.

Among the restored buildings in Heritage Canyon are a lovely small church, a one-room school, a general store, and other establishments and homes from the mid-1800s. A Christmas Walk is held in December with the village populated by citizens in appropriate costumes.

The Martin House Museum, managed by the Fulton Historical Society, is one of the few ante-bellum dwellings in town. Dr. Abraham Benton built the house in 1853. Besides being a physician, Dr. Benton and his wife were devoted spiritualists. After their deaths, the house was reported haunted, although no one seems to have encountered any ghosts.

The museum houses a collection of materials related to the history of Fulton and is open to the public only on Sunday (or at other times by appointment).

The Paddlewheel Pizza on Main Street is another favorite stop for bikers in need of a little refresher.

Sitting along Route 84 at the edge of Fulton is a large Shell truck stop where you can fuel up and grab some snacks and a soda.

Another stop you might want check out in Fulton is Freedom Motor Sports, whose slogan is "Your motorcycle connection." In addition to providing service for both foreign and domestic bikes, they also carry a full line of hard parts, accessories, and apparel. They are an authorized LEM dealer and also carry products from Skin Industries.

Roaring out of Fulton, a short jaunt will take you to the access road to Lock and Dam #13. An excellent blacktop winds along the backwaters of the Mississippi, a prime area for viewing waterfowl. Reaching the dam will give you a closer view of the barges, which regularly lock through.

In operation since 1994, Great River Road Antiques is a just few miles down the road and boasts the area's largest flea market. This five-acre bargain hunter's paradise is open every weekend from April through October from 9:00 a.m. to 5:00 p.m. Over fifty vendors display a surprising variety of merchandise.

After all the fresh air and exercise, you might be ready for a snack. Specialties include Amish jellies and candy, but be sure to try the gourmet pretzels available inside the mall.

The village of Thomson allows you get up-close-and-personal with the Mississippi at the Thomson Causeway Recreation Area. Situated in the Potter's Marsh Wildlife Area, the Class A Army Corps of Engineers campground offers 131 campsites, many right on the banks of the river. Most of the sites are on an island linked to the mainland by the causeway that gives the park its name.

A glimpse into the railroading past is available at the Thomson Depot Museum, typical of those built during the late 1800s and home to a collection of railroading memorabilia and historical records of the village. Admission is free; the museum opens Memorial Day weekend and is open on Friday, Saturday, and Sunday from 1:00 to 4:00 p.m. through September.

Complete your trip to Thomson with a stop at the McGinnis Market. This large open-air market has been a family-owned business for over one hundred years and features one of the finest selections of fresh fruits and vegetables available anywhere. They are particularly known for the quality of their homegrown melons available during the season. The market opens on Memorial Day weekend and is open through the fall season. Owners Randy and Cindy McGinnis are the third generation in the McGinnis family to operate the business.

The watermelon takes center stage on Labor Day Weekend when the village holds its annual Watermelon Days. A highlight of the festival is the chance to eat all the free watermelon you can hold.

There are two routes north out of Thomson: Route 84, which is the main highway, or the river road, a secondary blacktop which follows closely along the shoreline before cutting back to 84.

You can also turn east on the Argo Fay Road and head eight miles over to Route 78, a good road which runs parallel to Route 84. You can go north to Mount Carroll, or take a side trip south for about twelve miles to Damen Road. Here, a left turn takes you to the turnoff road to Morrison Rockwood State Park, or about a mile further down you come to a picturesque covered bridge. For those not wishing to camp, Morrison offers motels and the Hill N Dale B&B.

An abundance of autumn produce is displayed at McGinnis Market in Thomson, Illinois. The market opens on Memorial Day and remains open through the Fall.

Continuing the side trip to the east and south, if you take Route 78 out of Morrison you come to Prophetstown, a small town that celebrates its Native American heritage. At the time of the Black Hawk War, a large Indian settlement here was led by Chief White Cloud, a noted prophet, who gave the town its name. The site of the village is now the Prophetstown State Park. You can stop for a rest or camp on the banks of the Rock River. There is a historical museum on Main Street. In August 2005, the town dedicated the Eclipse Square Memorial Park honoring all vets and service men and women, along with monuments to police, firefighters, and emergency medical technicians.

Take 172 out of Prophetstown to the Tampico turnoff. In Tampico you can visit the birthplace of President Ronald Reagan or stop for the great food at the Dutch Diner, with their famous pies making the trip worthwhile. This is a stop on Reagan Trail.

The covered bridge over Rock Creek.

Follow Hahnaman Road out of Tampico to visit the Sandy Pine Elk Farm and Gift Shop near Deer Grove. You can take a tour of the elk pastures and see the bulls with their impressive antlers, and shop in the unique gift store that offers Northwoods décor and everything elk. The elk brats and burgers are excellent, as is their special Very Berry Pie. If you want less exotic fare, stop in Deer Grove at Arnie's Happy Spot for some of their special fried chicken. The local saying goes, "If the Colonel had used Arnie's recipe, he would have been a General."

Continue down Hahnaman road, then turn left on Route 40 into Rock Falls to Workman's Harley Davidson. You will be able to find all your Harley needs and a showroom full of new bikes and Harley merchandise.

Back on Route 40 you continue over the bridge and into Sterling. Take a right turn onto Route 2 and head through Sterling. You might enjoy a visit to the historic Dillon home or continue east to Sinnissippi Park.

A winding road overlooks the river, and the park makes a nice spot to take a break. The top of the bluff contains a group of Hopewellian Indian burial mounds.

Following Route 2 north you come to Dixon, where you can stop for a visit at the boyhood home of President Ronald Reagan. This is also part of the Reagan Trail which takes you south to the birthplace of the former president in Tampico and on down to Eureka where he graduated from Eureka College. There is also a Lincoln Memorial located along the river.

Another excellent stopping place in Dixon is Lowell Park, a state park, which includes Lowell Park Nature Center. As a young man of fifteen, Ronald Reagan started working at the park as a lifeguard. There is also a marker commemorating the Boles trail, an 1826 route used by pioneers traveling from Peoria to Galena.

Leaving Dixon, a short trek up the Rock River brings you to Grand Detour, which houses a museum dedicated to John Deere, the town's most famous resident. It was here in 1837 that Deere, a transplanted Vermonter, developed the plow that transformed agriculture in the Midwest.

Across from the entrance to the Deere Museum, a lovely little park alongside the river invites you to stop for a rest or a picnic.

Those who are interested in elegant food served in beautiful surroundings will want to stop at the Colonial Rose, which is also a Bed and Breakfast. The gourmet food prepared by owner/chef Jeff Rose and his wife Jayne make this not just a meal but also a fine dining experience. You might want to call ahead for reservations.

A leisurely ride up what has been called "one of the ten most scenic roads in the United States" brings you to Castle Rock State Park. If you feel the need to park the bikes and get some exercise you can take the trail to the top of the sandstone outcropping that gives the park its name. Once on top, you will have a spectacular view of the river valley below.

A statue of the young Abraham Lincoln is the centerpiece of the Lincoln Memorial in Dixon, Illinois.

Heading once more up the river, you arrive in the town of Oregon. A bridge across the river takes you to the road to Lowden State Park and a large Lorado Taft statue "The Eternal Indian." Familiarly known to locals as Black Hawk, the Sauk warrior gazes out across the river. Another fine view of the statue can be seen from the west side of the river just north of Oregon. You can enjoy a fine meal and an excellent view of the statue and river bluffs from the dining room at Maxson Riverside Restaurant. The Sunday Champagne Brunch is well worth the trip. For another perspective try the view from the deck of the Pride of Oregon Riverboat which offers river cruises and has its home dock beside the restaurant. Luxury accommodations are available at the Paddlewheel Inn.

A statue of John Deere at work at his anvil is on display at the John Deere Historical Site in Grand Detour.

The first weekend in October, Oregon braces for an influx of visitors during the Autumn on Parade festival. The town square and side streets are lined with crafters and food stands and a rendezvous with re-enactors is held on the east side of the river. Farther north up Route 2, a Renaissance Fair is held on the grounds of Stronghold Castle, which was built on a scenic bluff overlooking the river. The castle is open for tours at this time.

The town of Byron celebrates its colorful history by preserving the Lucius Read House, now The Byron Museum of History, which was once a safe house for escaping slaves on the underground railroad

At Byron, you can cross the river for a pretty drive down the east shore or continue up the Rock and cross just below Rockford. You then follow down the east side to Lowden State park from the north..

Bud Scamardo of Rochelle, Illinois, parks his Harley Davidson FLHATCUI Electroglide Classic while his wife Renetta sets up a picnic lunch at the riverside park in Grand Detour.

Crossing the bridge back to Oregon take Pines Road west, but be sure to stop in at LaDonna Family Campground. A beach open to the public beckons hot travelers for a relaxing swim and many activities are centered around two raised Tahitian huts. You might want to visit the Vietnam Veterans Memorial that is also on the grounds.

A trip of about eight miles west on Pines Road takes you to White Pines State Park, one of the nicest in the area. Special features of the park include a forty-three-acre nature preserve protecting one of the last stands of virgin white pine trees in Illinois. Also protected are Canada yew and Sullivantia, two rare breeds of plants that are found in the dolomite cliffs.

"The Eternal Indian," a fifty-foot-tall monolith with a six-foot base, watches over the Rock River at Lowden State Park. Lorado Taft sculpted the statue, with help from John G. Prasuhn.

Two concrete fords across the creek also are still in use, although bikers must use care and expect wet feet.

Besides the many campsites, there are also several modern log cabins and the White Pines Inn, which houses a restaurant, gift shop, and dinner theater, and which also offers 13 one-room cabins and three larger cabins available for rent.

A special cabin package provides you with lodging, meals and discounted tickets to a performance at the theater. Many other package deals including a special romantic get-away are offered.

Six miles further along on Pines Road you come to the town of Polo, which has several historic buildings overseen by the Polo Historical Society. These include the Burns house, once the home of a Polo doctor, and the Henry School. An interesting visit may also be made to the Aplington House Museum. In June Polo holds its traditional Town and Country Days festival.

Highway 52 north out of Polo links you with Highway 64, which will bring you into Mount Carroll from the east. Built among the rolling hills, Mount Carroll is known for its historic homes and its friendly atmosphere.

The Civil War Monument sitting at the corner of the courthouse square is topped by a Lorado Taft sculpture. Carroll County boasts a total of one thousand four hundred thirty-one men who fought for the Union in the Civil War. This is also listed in Guinness Book of World Records as the only Civil War Monument with an annex that was added to include all the names of the Civil War Veterans.

You might enjoy a self-guided walking tour of the many buildings in the National Register Historic District.

The Mayfest Celebration is held over Memorial Day weekend and provides entertainment, arts and crafts, a walk-run, a car show, and a beer-wine garden.

Campbell Learning Center, at the former home of Shimer College, was established in 1979 as a non-profit educational complex. This center trains persons working in the fields of historic architectural preservation, collections care, conservation, and historic landscapes.

Just south of Mount Carroll is the Timber Lake Resort and Campground. In existence since 1955, Timber Lake offers 250 acres of natural beauty. Whether you wish to camp, prefer to rest in the luxury of the recently added log cabins or merely stop for a quiet picnic lunch, the relaxed atmosphere allows you to rest and recharge.

The Civil War Memorial on Courthouse Square in Mount Carroll.

For campers looking for some off-bike activities, there are a newly-constructed in-ground swimming pool and canoe and paddleboats rentals. You might also wish to visit the nearby Oakville golf course.

The Oakville complex includes log cabins, a schoolhouse, a granary, and a blacksmith shop (open only by appointment).

A popular attraction is the adjacent Timber Lake Playhouse for those who enjoy live theater. Beginning in 1961, Timber Lake Playhouse is the oldest continuously operating summer stock theater in Illinois, where throughout the summer a semi-professional company mounts several excellent productions including musicals, comedies, and intense dramas.

Route 78 north out of Mount Carroll brings you to the most scenic part of Illinois, with absolutely beautiful country. If you opt to stay on Highway 84, Buck's Barn, located a few miles north of Thomson, is a great place to stop and have a meal. The restaurant, in a renovated old barn, features an outstanding menu with excellent food. Next to the restaurant are a motel and a golf course.

A group of bikers wind down a hill on Scenic Ridge Road north of Mount Carroll

As you head to the north, the scenery begins to change. The bluffs which were always in the distance become closer and suddenly start to look higher. When you pull up to the stop sign at the outskirts of Savanna, you suddenly are facing a limestone bluff topped by a large motel.

Savanna acts as a hub for several loop excursions. You can leave the town in any direction and find great scenery and excellent roads. East on Highway 64 a short jaunt will take you to the town of Mount Carroll, and the road west takes you across the bridge into Iowa and the island town of Sabula. Traveling north takes you to the breathtaking views from Mississippi Palisades State

Park. Or head northeast to the town of Elizabeth for one of the most beautiful rides in the Midwest.

The downtown area of Savanna is wedged into a narrow strip between the bluffs to the east and the Mississippi to the west. Main Street has two businesses that are geared specifically toward bikers: "Poopy's Motorcycle Parts and Accessories" and "Poopy's Pub" (located in a basement) are major stops for riders, and on the weekends the parking spaces are packed with bikes. The riders enjoy the friendly atmosphere of the establishment, and on weekends the place really gets hopping.

On weekends bikers converge on Poopy's on Savanna's Main Street. The retail store features a full line of Harley merchandise, and the basement pub and adjacent tattoo parlor are also popular attractions.

Upstairs a tattoo parlor in an adjoining room allows you to choose from a wide selection of body art or (if you wish) you might opt for a piercing.

The retail shop features a full line of Harley clothing and accessories, as well as a full line of Harley and aftermarket parts at reduced prices and some cruiser parts.

A certified Harley mechanic is available at the full service repair shop, although they will work on all brands for service parts. Poopy's soon will be moving to a new location south of Savanna on 84. The expanded business will include a restaurant, outdoor stage, beer garden, and free tent camping.

The other weekend hot spot is "The Iron Horse Social Club," and you can come away wishing for a four-day weekend instead of just Friday, Saturday, and Sunday. Live bands rock the windows on Saturday and Sunday. While visiting there, you will want to check out the great collection of racing bikes that owner Jerry Gendreau has on display throughout the premises.

The Pulford Opera House, which houses northwestern Illinois' largest antique mall, is a beautiful example of the opulent architecture of one hundred years ago or more. Many fine Victorian homes and a number of commercial buildings also tell of the town's prosperous past.

Catering to boats and motorcycles, Looney Linda's Bar and Restaurant plans to have rooftop dining and a tiki bar overlooking the Mississippi. Harvest Moon Emporium features antiques, gourmet foods and fine decorative accessories. Of particular interest to chocoholics is The Candy Store, located on the premises. Cherokee Junction is also an interesting place to stop, a store featuring antiques, baseball cards, and gifts.

For those wishing a longer stay in Savanna there is a wide selection of overnight accommodations and eateries.

Just north of town on Highway 84 you skirt the high rocky outcroppings at Mississippi Palisades State Park.

The park features spectacular lookouts from the top of the bluffs. A short distance inside the main entrance of the park is a right turn onto a side road that heads to the south end of the park, winding up bluffs and down into the valleys. The main route through the park takes you up a steep and curvy road to the four lookout points at the top, then snakes down to the modern campground.

Two of the antique racing bikes on display in the motorcycle museum at the Iron Horse Social Club in downtown Savanna.

The artesian well at the south entrance to Mississippi Palisades State Park is a great place to stop and fill your water bottles.

Brave riders may leave Savanna and cross the metal-floored bridge to Sabula, Iowa. As you head across the bridge the open grid of the bridge floor allows you to look down at the moving water. Or you may continue north on 84. However, a ride that should not be missed is the back road through the hills to the town of Elizabeth. This trip, starting on Webster Street, is one of the most beautiful rides in the entire state of Illinois.

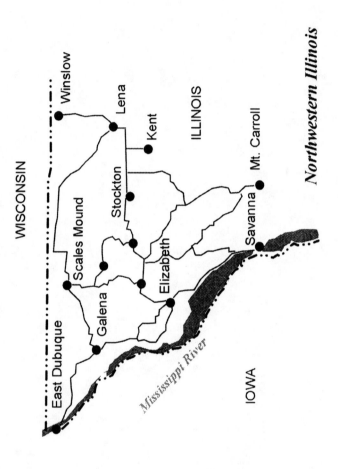

CHAPTER TWO

HILLS AND CURVES AT THE TOP OF ILLINOIS

For those who have not traveled its byways, it is difficult to imagine the beauty of the country in the Northwestern corner of Illinois. The roads traverse high hills and ridges overlooking peaceful farmlands. The area includes Northern Carroll County and the spectacular Jo Daviess and Stephenson Counties. Here you will find Charles Mound, the highest point in the state along with the historic town of Galena and the lovely village of Elizabeth. Twisting and climbing along the many excellent back roads will give you an awesome riding experience.

Webster Street in Savanna is a steep trail to the top of the bluffs overlooking the town. Webster soon turns into Scenic Ridge Road and then heads north toward Jo Daviess County, a sparkling jewel at the top of Illinois.

A day or more spent exploring the pastoral beauty of this area can refresh the spirit and calm the soul. However, you must exercise caution, since the roads curve in all directions and mostly swoop up and down, with only an occasional straight, flat stretch along a valley floor.

As it winds through hilly farmland, the Scenic Ridge Road changes to Derinda Road at the Jo Daviess County line. It would be easy to get whiplash along here as you try to glimpse the scenery in all directions, while still attempting to pay attention to riding your bike. This is a good time to hang onto your hats and your handlebars.

The high hills give panoramic views of the neat farms and mosaic patterns of fields dotted with small ponds and livestock. This ride is gorgeous at any time of the year but the fall colors make it truly breathtaking.

This road also can be accessed from Route 78 just north of Mount Carroll where you can turn onto the Elizabeth blacktop to wind over to Derinda Road, or continue north on 78 for a pleasant ride.

A short side trip off Derinda Road on Massbach Road will take you to the tiny town of Massbach, home to a newly-opened winery. Like most of the roads in northwestern Illinois, Massbach Road is also very scenic with more fantastic views from the top of the ridges.

Acres of vineyards surround the Massbach Ridge Winery.

Swinging back to your main course you will reach Route 20 just east of the lovely hamlet of Elizabeth.

Of particular interest in Elizabeth is the Apple River Fort State Historic Site. This reconstructed fort commemorates the brave defense of the village by the settlers against a large war-party lead by the warrior Black Hawk of the Sac tribe during the 1832 Black Hawk War. Believing that the white man had cheated his people, Black Hawk led his warriors in a rampage throughout northern Illinois and into Wisconsin before finally being defeated. An interpretive center gives a glimpse into the attitudes of the times.

The reconstructed Apple River Fort commemorates the battle where forty-five settlers including men, women, and children held off two hundred warriors under Black Hawk.

Another top attraction is the Chicago Great Western Railway Depot Museum located on East Myrtle Street. The Museum tells the story of Elizabeth and the

Railroad. Those with a taste for fine pottery can visit Eshelmann's Pottery or stop at Studio Works to see the creator, Adrienne Seagraves.

The buildings inside walls of the Apple River Fort demonstrate the living conditions of the early 1800s.

Georgetown Bridge, crossing the Apple River on the northwest side of town, was built in 1892. The three spans of this iron bridge cross over abutments and piers constructed of native limestone.

You might also enjoy a visit to Bishop's Busy Big Store where there has been little change over the last fifty years.

Just at the edge of town is the Elizabeth/Scales Mound Road, which leads north into the hills. This scenic byway rivals Derinda Road in its beauty and excellence. Take time to explore its curves. This road is popular with bikers and is equally scenic whether you travel it from the north or the south.

Highway 20 west takes you across Terrapin Ridge and to several roadside parks, one featuring a wooden tower where you can take a break and climb up for an even more spectacular view of the countryside.

From a lookout point on Route 20 the village of Elizabeth is seen nestled in the hills.

Continuing on Route 20 northwest you will come to the historic town of Galena. Be aware, however, that on this highway you will have to contend with heavy truck traffic. Although the higher hills do have slow lanes, you'll still need to be extremely cautious.

Another excellent ride takes you south from the junction of Routes 20 and 84 to the town of Hanover, billed as the Mallard Capital of the World. Events here include the Mallard Fest held the third Saturday in September. On July 3, the town hosts fireworks over the Apple River, a parade, and canoe races.

The concrete railings and arched supports of the Route 84 Bridge over the Apple River are very close replicas of ornamentation included on the original bridge built in 1934. If you look just below the bridge, you are treated to the sight of Apple River Falls, formed by a natural ledge in the bedrock. The water tumbling down eleven feet has provided, with the help of dams, power for saw, grist, and woolen mills.

Blackjack Road out of Hanover takes you west to the Chestnut Mountain Resort. This is a full service resort, with a motel, spa, restaurant, and many activities to entertain you.

During the winter there is great skiing down the challenging runs and six chair lifts offer easy trips back to the top.

One chair lift is in operation at all times during the summer and a ride down and back up gives you a spectacular three state view in addition to the river vistas. For a breathtaking visual treat ride the ski lift when the fall colors are at their height.

Other summer activities allow you to hurtle down the bluff on the Alpine Slide, try your hand at mini golf or volleyball, rent a mountain bike or simply hike the many trails.

On the second weekend in September, Triumph riders use Chestnut Mountain as the base for a large road rally. The riders enjoy a poker run around the scenic roads and use the large parking lot to display hundreds of bikes.

If you wish to extend your stay, the complex offers several indoor activities, including a swimming pool, whirlpool, lounges, and fine dining, with live entertainment featured on weekends.

A couple of miles further along, a discrete sign leads you to the Goldmoor Inn. This luxury inn features the finest in lodging and special holiday packages and has been listed as one of the twelve most romantic inns in North America. This is a motorcycle-friendly spot, and many riders trailer their bikes in and then tour the countryside. Among the special services provided by owners Jim and Pat Goldthorpe is housing the bikes in the garages for the night. Calling on his twelve years as a tour guide, plus having grown up in the area, Jim is a fountain of unique information concerning the area.

A group of bikers wind their way up from the valley on Route 20.

Back on the trail, Blackjack Road finishes its sixteen-mile loop and brings you into Galena from the west.

The town of Galena, a former lead mining town, is located on the Galena River. The top of the dike is an excellent place for a picnic lunch. Although the river is now a gently flowing stream, at least most of the time, at one time Galena was the busiest port between St. Louis, Missouri and St. Paul, Minnesota. This is reflected in the many mansions built in the town during the 1800s. Galena is a treasure trove of classic architectural styles.

Be sure to notice the huge floodgates that protect the lower section of the town during high water. And please pay attention to the "duck-crossing" signs; they aren't a joke.

The lookout tower at the rest area on Route 20 gives a panoramic view of the surrounding valleys.

The town itself is built on a series of steep hills, and one of the first things you notice is that instead of sidewalks between the sections of town there are steps, so exploring the town takes endurance. However, if you prefer a less strenuous tour, you can visit the Galena Trolley Depot and take a one-hour narrated and guided non-stop journey through the town. You can also opt for a more extended tour, which will include visiting a three-and-one-half acre private garden and a stop at the home of President Ulysses S. Grant.

The picturesque arched supports of the Route 84 bridge are reflected in the Apple River at Hanover.

As a young man, Grant worked in the leather shop belonging to his family. The house was presented to him by the proud and respectful townspeople when he returned to his hometown in 1865 as a general and a hero of the Civil War. The handsome brick home is now a state historic site and still contains much of Grant's original furniture.

The Mississippi River is shown in all its glory from the ski lifts at Chestnut Mountain Resort.

For a comprehensive history of the area, a visit to the Jo Daviess County Historical Society and Museum is recommended. Here you will see the original of Thomas Nast's famous painting "Peace in the Union" which depicts Lee surrendering to Grant at Appomattox. At nine feet by twelve feet, the work was too big to be brought in through the doors and instead entered through the large windows.

The museum also houses several other paintings, a large landform model explaining how the glaciers spared the area, several historical exhibits, and an award winning slide show. There is also a museum gift and bookshop. During renovations, an old lead mine was discovered under the building, and you can look down into the mine from inside the building.

Galena is built into a series of steep hills making it necessary to use steps rather than regular sidewalks to go between levels.

For more history of the area you can visit Belvedere House and Gardens, Galena's largest mansion. This was originally the home of steamship owner J. Russell Jones, who later served as ambassador to Belgium. This house contains one of the finest collections of Victorian antiques in the country. Also open to the public is Galena's oldest home, the Dowling House, which started as a primitive dwelling and was an old miner's trading post.

Among other spots to visit, The Old Market House holds a permanent collection of Grant memorabilia and also houses an information center. The blacksmith shop provides an interesting look into the past.

Another stop for bikers is the Galena Bridge Branch of Wilwert's Harley Davidson/Buell Shop. They have a full selection of gear and repair parts. The main headquarters is located in Dubuque, Iowa.

When it is time to eat, the challenging choice of 30 restaurants awaits you. Those in the know say it is impossible to find a bad meal in the town.

Another popular activity is browsing among the eighty-five quaint shops located in the downtown area and up and down the surrounding streets.

If you plan a longer visit, you'll find that many of the former mansions have been transformed into bed and breakfasts. Galena is also graced by a number of fine motels and hotels.

From downtown Galena you can hook up with another road to Scales Mound, which takes you up to join the Stagecoach Trail. Weaving its way across the top of Illinois just below the Wisconsin border, it follows the old mail route that once linked the village of Chicago to the bustling metropolis of Galena.

Charles Mound, the highest point in Illinois at one thousand two hundred thirty-five feet above sea level is located in this area. The mound itself is on private land, and you must gain permission before visiting the site.

The ornate Victorian façade of Belvedere House is quite striking.

Here, too, you will find Scales Mound, the "town at the top of Illinois." In 1990 virtually the entire town was placed on the National Registry of Historic Places. Among the points of interest is the former James Allen Warehouse now housing Countryside Feeds. Built in the 1860s, the second floor of this unique structure once contained an opera house and the community hall. Country House Grocery has been in continuous operation as a grocery store since 1859.

Scales Mound, the hill that gives the town its name, sits a mile southwest and is now maintained by one of the local churches. A large flat rock with the words "Jesus Saves" now occupies the spot where Samuel Scales built a tavern in 1830.

Straight south of Scales Mound, you can catch the north end of the gorgeous Elizabeth/Scales Mound Road. This road is wonderful coming from the south, but even more spectacular heading down from the north.

Any side road branching off Stagecoach Trail will take you through lovely hills and valleys, but a trip down Scout Camp Road will be worth your time. You can get on Scout Camp directly from Stagecoach Trail, but the road is fairly straight on the north end. Taking the Elizabeth/Scales Mound road south and then cutting across on the scenic Schapville Road can provide a more challenging ride. You will come out on Scout Camp just south of Apple Canyon Lake. Turn south for a fun ride down to the village of Woodbine.

When taking Scout Camp Road between Woodbine and Schapville Road, be very alert. The road is full of sharp twists and (like most of the back roads in Jo Daviess County) does not have any guardrails.

If you decide to remain on Stagecoach Trail, continue east to Warren. This town also sports many buildings listed on the National Register of Historic Places. The Warren Historical Society Museum occupies the building that was built in 1895 to house the village fire department and pump station.

The Greek Revival style of architecture is reflected in the entryway and cornice returns of the Warren Community Building which was built as a hotel in 1852 by Freeman Tisdell.

From Warren you dip down to the town of Nora, the smallest village in Jo Daviess County.

Just outside of Nora you cross into Stephenson County and head over to the town of Lena. A couple miles north of town on Lake Road is Lake Le-Aqua-Na State Park. A snake-like trail circles the lake. Signs giving directions to the park are prominently displayed as you enter the town.

A panoramic view of the countryside is seen from the road just outside of the hamlet of Schapville.

After completing the circuit of the lake you come back out on Lake Road and a left turn takes you around to Route 73.

A rewarding side trip would be to continue on 73 North to the village of Winslow. Keep a close watch as you enter town, and you will see a sign directing you to an artesian well. This is very easy to miss, as you must pull behind the Grace Free Bible Church. Paradise Cove, a small city park, has been built around the well. A large water wheel, a covered footbridge over the creek, and a man-made waterfall are features of the park. Be sure to bring your water bottles so you can sample the pure spring water that flows from the well at 444 gallons per minute.

The Winslow River Days Celebration is held in the town during the second weekend of August.

Danny Anderson and Diane Solis stop their Harleys to admire the waterfall at Paradise Cove in Winslow.

Heading back down Route 73, you may now be hungry for a snack and a good place to stop would be the Torkelson Cheese Factory a few miles north of Lena on

Route 73. You definitely will enjoy sampling the award-winning cheeses on sale at the factory shop.

Continuing south, you will connect with Highway 20 about two miles south of Lena and take a turn back west. Before leaving Lena, however, you might want to glance at the 125-foot Historic Water Tower which is still in use and was built of limestone and brick in 1896.

A few miles out of Lena along Highway 20, a left turn onto Kent Road will take you to Monument Road where the road turns to gravel, but it is worth the mile-and-a-half trip to visit the Black Hawk War Memorial. A small cemetery and a tall monument mark the spot where a small group of soldiers was ambushed and killed by Black Hawk and his warriors. The day after the battle, a company of soldiers arrived to help the few survivors bury the fallen men. Among those helping with the burial duties was a young soldier named Abraham Lincoln. In addition to a great view, you also will find an authentic log cabin and a nice picnic shelter.

Returning to the blacktop, a right turn will take you to the village of Kent whose welcome sign boasts a population of seventy people and forty-eight dogs. Or you can head back up to Route 20 west and about a mile down the road find the conveniently located Kolb-Lena Cheese Company. At the outlet shop, cheese lovers may choose among the specialties of the house, including Delico Baby Swiss, Saladena Feta, Montrachet Goat Cheese, New Holland Havarti, and Ile de France Brie, as well as Camembert, Alouette Baby Brie, and Alouette Crème de Brie. The cheese shop is open Monday through Saturday from 10:00 a.m. to 6:00 p.m. and on Sundays from 9:00 a.m. to 5:00 p.m.

After making your selections from among the fine cheeses, you continue west to just before the town of Stockton and a trip down Willow Road. This byway takes you through an exquisite little valley and past a small country church where each year the Willow Folk Festival is held on the second full weekend in August. Here you can enjoy the folk-style music by the best amateur musicians in Northern Illinois, or it is worth visiting the festival just to sample their famous pies.

Continuing down Willow Road to Highway 78, you'll see a sign reading "Willow Inn B&B, Motorcycles Welcome." Even if you don't plan to spend the night, it is worth it to drive back and meet Chris and Sue Rogers. Chris is an avid motorcyclist and loves nothing more than leading a group of guests on a ride around the area. The Inn itself is in a beautiful setting along the banks of a winding creek offering three tasteful, non-smoking guest rooms, plus a sun porch that can double as a bedroom.

The Willow Inn Bed & Breakfast caters to motorcyclists. Owner Chris Rogers is always happy to lead bikers on a tour of the area.

After a short jog of about a mile north on Highway 78, you can turn off on Bethel Road. This fun ride of hills and sweepers will complete a loop tour that brings you back once again to Route 20 just east of Elizabeth. Or you may wish to continue north to Stockton, where you will find the Stockton Cheese Plant, the original home built in 1914 of the J.L. Kraft cheese factory. Although now under different ownership, the plant still produces more Swiss cheese than any other factory in America. Unfortunately, tours of this facility are not offered, but artifacts from the Kraft cheese plant, along with other items of local interest, are on display at the Stockton Historical Museum which is housed in the restored Niemeyer Drugstore, circa 1908.

Route 20 heading west is another alternate, but heavily traveled, road to Elizabeth.

If on your previous visit you chose one of the alternative routes from Elizabeth to Galena, you might now wish to take Route 20 for a straight shot north and west. This provides a roller coaster ride up steep inclines and then sudden drops down to the valley floor.

The Galena Territory, an upscale housing and recreation area, includes the Eagle Ridge Resort and Spa. Hot air balloon rides are available here, although they must be booked in advance.

Just north of Galena, a fork in the road forces a decision. Do you head to Hazel Green, Wisconsin up Highway 84 or stay on 20 West? You can put off the need to choose for a few more miles by staying on 20 and going over to the town of East Dubuque. Here you go either north into Grant County, Wisconsin or cross the Mississippi River over into Iowa.

If you decide to head up Route 84, you will come to the turnoff to the Vinegar Hill Lead Mine and Museum. Here a guide will explain early mining methods, and you will get an idea of the harsh conditions endured by the miners. The museum displays the primitive tools used in working the mine and also many artifacts indigenous to the area.

Shortly after crossing the state line into Wisconsin, you can make a left turn onto Sinsinawa Road. This well-paved but narrow road provides some nice curves and small hills before bringing you out at the Sinsinawa Mound Center.

Following Route 20 East you come to the town of East Dubuque.

A jaunt to the top of the bluff overlooking the Mississippi River will reward you with Gramercy Park, three acres of land containing walking trails and twenty-six Indian mounds from the Hopewell Indian culture. The Hopewell Indians occupied the Upper Mississippi Valley roughly from 300 B.C. to 500 A.D.

Words of warning here: When traveling into Illinois from the north, avoid East Dubuque on Sunday afternoons. This is a traffic bottleneck. You can spend several hours inching along for a couple of miles.

You can't really go wrong with either Route 20 or 84, for both lead to places that have much to offer the biker. We will check them out in subsequent chapters.

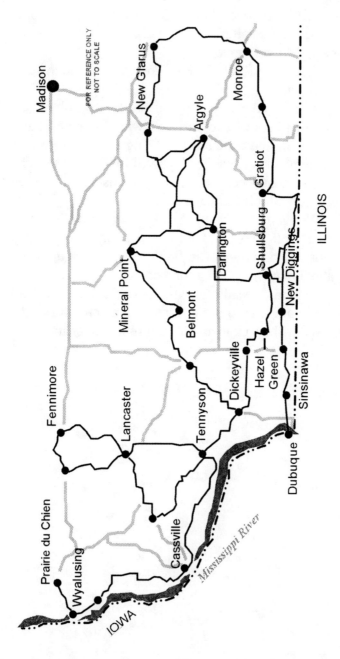

The wonderland of southwestern Wisconsin

CHAPTER THREE

WISCONSIN WONDERLAND

From the peace and inspiration of Sinsinawa Mound, to the cheese capital of Monroe and north to around Route 18, southwestern Wisconsin will offer you both fun rides and excellent food. This is a dream area for cheese lovers with local varieties available around each corner and over each hill. If you wish to sample other delicacies, you can visit one of several small breweries, try an authentic Cornish pasty at Mineral Point, or make a pit stop in the motorcycle Mecca of New Diggings. Wisconsin is well known for its excellent county roads, which are an absolute joy for bikers. The state designates them "County Trunk Highway," and assigns them letters instead of numbers, so bikers call them "alphabet roads." For convenience, they will be abbreviated to CTH in the Wisconsin chapters that follow.

Route 35 north takes you from East Dubuque and over the line into Wisconsin's Grant County. Your trip to the east starts with a right turn onto Highway 11. Another right turn onto County Road Z brings you to

Sinsinawa Mound and the home of the Sinsinawa Dominicans.

At Sinsinawa, all visitors are welcome to walk the indoor or outdoor labyrinths and experience a sense of peace and tranquility. The Dominican Sisters are famous for their bakery and their cinnamon bread, caramel rolls, and other mouth-watering treats which should come with warning labels stating "Highly Addictive Substance." They are available at the gift shop, open Monday through Saturday from 10:00 a.m. to 5:00 p.m. from April 1st to November 30th. From December 1st to March 31st, they are closed on Mondays. Fresh bakery items arrive at the gift shop at noon each day.

The impressive Sinsinawa Mound has been home to the Dominican Sisters for over one hundred fifty years.

Father Samuel Mazzuchelli, who founded churches in many of the towns and did so much to spread the gospel in Southern Wisconsin, founded this religious order.

The short loop down CTH Z is a beautiful ride, even if you decide not to visit the bakery.

From Sinsinawa you once again catch Highway 11 and continue east to the town of Hazel Green. This is also the first Wisconsin town you encounter when traveling up Route 84, which becomes Route 80 at the Wisconsin line.

Hazel Green is known as Wisconsin's "Point of Beginning." Just outside of town an historical marker designates the spot where the first land surveys began in 1831. Several historic buildings remain in the town, including the Wisconsin House built in 1846 and the Opera House/Town Hall that went up in 1898. You might also wish to visit the town's antique shops.

Winding through the bluffs of Southern Wisconsin, CTH W is a biker's delight.

Due east out of Hazel Green, CTH W takes you through the hills to one of the most popular and well known motorcycle haunts in southern Wisconsin, the tiny town of New Diggings. The two main businesses are the

New Diggings General Store and Anton's Saloon, home of the macho burger.

Both of the buildings have a "Wild West" appearance, and on any given weekend you can find many bikes filling the parking lots, parked alongside of the buildings and lining the streets.

A major weekend biker attraction is Anton's Saloon in New Diggings.

Here also is the St. Augustine Catholic Church built in 1884. As Wisconsin's oldest Catholic Church and the only remaining wooden church built by Father Mazzuchelli, this treasure has been added to the National Register of Historic Places.

CTH W takes you over to catch CTH O and a north turn to Shullsburg which sets on Highway 11. Like many of the area towns, Shullsburg owes its existence to lead mining, which is reflected in the Badger Mine and Museum where you can take a guided tour through the one-half-mile main passageway. A visit to the museum will acquaint you with early farm tools and medical equipment. The museum also houses a general store, a drugstore, a tobacco shop, a turn-of-the-century kitchen, a blacksmith shop, and a carpenter's shop.

Three unique dining areas and Shullsburg's finest cheese are available at the Brewster Café and Cheese Store.

Also be sure to visit Gravity Hill where cars and bikes roll uphill in defiance of the natural laws of science.

The Badger Mine and Museum located in the eight acre Badger Park takes you back to the days when miners labored forty-five feet below ground to mine the lead by hand. Picks, gads, and blasting powder were their only tools.

West of Shullsburg, a pretty drive down Highway 11 leads you to Benton, and the first thing you notice as you approach the town is the stone-based water tower erected in 1899. The historic St. Patrick's Catholic Church was one of the last structures built by Father Mazzuchelli; his rectory has been restored and moved close to its original site, and his grave is also close by.

For those interested in the not-so-saintly citizens, a visit to the Swindler's Ridge Museum might prove interesting. This museum was named after a nearby ridge where unscrupulous miners stole lead from each other's diggings. It is open weekends from noon to 4:00 p.m. from Memorial Day to Labor Day.

The Village School House Museum is located in the original schoolhouse, which was built in 1851. It houses records of alumni and memorabilia from the village history.

A trip up CTH J will take you to Cuba City, "The City of the Presidents." The water tower is painted red, white, and blue, and red, white and blue shields, one for each president, line the main street. This display began in

1976 as a community Bicentennial project. The annual "The Parade of Presidents" is recognized as the longest ongoing Bicentennial project in the United States.

The patriotic water tower is located in Splinter Park, a great place to stop for a picnic lunch. Before heading to the park, it is a good idea to stop at Gile Cheese Store, famous since 1946 for its high-quality merchandise. Among other items are the fifteen varieties of cheese produced by Carr Cheese Factory just outside of Cuba City. Despite being one of Wisconsin's smallest cheese plants, their products have won many awards.

Once you have made your selection of cheeses, the next stop should be Weber's Processing Plant where you can chose delectable meats. Weber's on-site butchering facility assures that any meat purchased at the full-service meat counter is fresh and tasty. But if you are more in the mood for a sit down meal, the Café on the Main offers great food in a casual atmosphere.

When you are ready to move on again, CTH Roads H and HH will take you west over to Dickeyville. A second option for leaving Shullsburg is to continue north on CTH O. This road is winding and very hilly. You will want to hang onto your stomachs as you climb up and drop down on this roller coaster ride. Stay on O until you reach the historic Cornish settlement of Mineral Point (more about this village later).

For a third choice, you may head southeast out of Shullsburg following CTH A down until it hits CTH W, then going east until you connect with Highway 78 North. A left turn takes you to the town of Gratiot. A nice side loop to the east takes you to Browntown-Cadiz Springs recreation area, a lovely small park that invites you to take a break for rest and relaxation. Be advised, though; Wisconsin State Parks do require a user's fee. Feeling relaxed, you now can head on east to the town of Monroe.

A good place to start your tour of the town is the Monroe Depot, built in 1880's and moved to its present location at Highway 69 South and 21st Street. A visit to the information center will be very helpful in planning your visit. The Depot also houses a Historic Cheesemaking Center where you can learn about the history of making cheese and get information on the forty-seven-mile-long Cheese Country Recreation Trail.

Honeybelle the cow greets visitors at the Monroe Depot, which houses the Historic Cheesemaking Center and a tourist information site.

Monroe is truly the heart of cheese country. Not only is it famous for its Swiss cheeses, it also is the only place in the United States that still produces Limburger cheese. If this piques your curiosity and taste buds, you might consider swinging by Baumgartner's on the town square and ordering a Limburger sandwich. Since 1931, Baumgartner's has featured an "almost world famous menu."

In mid-September of even-numbered years the annual Cheese Days celebrate the town's Swiss heritage and its historic cheesemaking industry. This is rated as one of the top one hundred festivals in the United States.

A visit to the Green County Historical Museum is also interesting. On display you will find many antique cheesemaking utensils, along with memorabilia from the Civil War. The Museum was built in 1861 and formerly housed a Universalist Church and features lovely stained glass windows dating back to the 1890's.

You might also enjoy a Taster's Tour of the Joseph Huber Brewery, the oldest continuously operating brewery in Wisconsin and the second oldest in the United States. Huber has been producing fine beer since 1845 except during the years of Prohibition. Tours are conducted every two hours starting at 11:00 a.m. to 3:00 p.m. on Thursday, Friday, and Saturday.

The unique, Romanesque-style Green County Courthouse is worth a stop. This structure was built in 1891; two State Supreme Court Justices helped pound in mortar while laying the cornerstone. Two rare murals by Berlin artist Franz Rohrbeck grace the Circuit Court on the second floor.

If specialty treats are more to your liking, mouth-watering delicacies abound at the Swiss Colony and its outlet store. Since 1926, this company has been selling marvelous cheeses along with bakery and chocolate items guaranteed to satisfy the most rabid sweet tooth. Another site you might wish to visit is Twining Park, named after General Twining who was a Monroe native. On permanent display at the park is an F-86 sabre jet.

The famous Green County Courthouse has stood since 1891 as a tribute to the ornate Romanesque-style architecture.

A trip up Highway 69 North brings you to the town of New Glarus, located in the area known as America's Little Switzerland.

Settled in 1845 by a group of 108 Swiss pioneers, the town celebrates its Swiss heritage with the Wilhelm Tell Festival held every year in September, a pageant honoring the famous archer first held sixty-six years ago. The town also holds an annual Oktoberfest.

Other points of interest in the town include the Historical Swiss Village where you can enjoy a look into pioneer life. There are fourteen buildings, each one representing a facet of life on what was then the western frontier. The Village is open daily from May to October. Start your visit at the Hall of History, then continue through the settlement.

The New Glarus Brewing Company produces seven year-round beers, two bock beers, five seasonal brews to complement the different holidays, and a selection of surprises, and is the only brewery that was founded by a woman, Deborah Carey. Her husband, Dan, is the brewmaster. Since it is a small microbrewery, their product is distributed only in Wisconsin but for those who appreciate a fine beer or ale, a visit to the brewery is a must. Self-guided tours are held from 10:30 a.m. to 4:30 p.m. Monday through Friday, and guided tours are held on Saturdays during the summer months. You will also want to visit the tasting room and gift shop.

A stop at the Primrose Winery for a free tasting of some of their thirteen wines also is recommended, or you might wish to spend some time investigating the many unique shops and restaurants that are located in the town.

From New Glarus you swing onto County H to Blanchardville, the smallest town in the state to earn the prestigious Wisconsin Main Street Community designation. The Blanchardville Historical Society Museum on Main Street offers a look into the community's past; you can pick up a brochure that includes a walking tour of the town's historic buildings. Blanchardville also marks the northern gateway to Yellowstone Lake State Park where CTH F, G, and N circle the park.

Every evening the 455-acre lake and the surrounding wildlife area take a back seat to the real entertainment, which is watching the bats. You also will notice the welcome absence of mosquitoes in the park. This is because each of the approximately 4000 brown bats in residence eats up to 600 mosquitoes an hour. This natural method of control has virtually wiped out the mosquito population in this area and does much to debunk the fear that all bats carry rabies. At dusk the campers gather near the bat houses to watch nature's air show as the bats swoop and dive, hunting their suppers.

Argyle, to the east of Yellowstone Lake, gives one an opportunity to visit the miniature world of The Toy Train Barn. There are many hands-on activities here, where you can see an operating sawmill or load an ore car with coal. You can also take a ride on the outdoor park train, the Argyle Zephyr.

If you are in Argyle on a Friday evening, you might like to stop in at the Partridge Hall Banquet and Lodging for their Famous Friday Fish Fry. This turn-of-the-century inn offers fine dining and has two guest rooms each fashioned with period décor.

Continue on F to Darlington where you might enjoy a visit to the Lafayette County Historical Society and Depot Museum. The Historical Society Museum is located in the former Darlington Public Library and displays a large collection of Kammerude paintings, along with medical displays, old photography equipment, and old time barbering and hairdressing salons, plus a compilation of genealogical records which are open to the public.

The Depot Museum houses railroad memorabilia, model trains, old railroad maps, and oil paintings of the Lafayette County depots by Florence Bennet.

Or you could take CTH G over to Route 23 and turn north for a visit to Mineral Point, one of the oldest communities in Wisconsin. Mineral Point is a historic village that was settled by miners from Cornwall in England. Route 23 between the two towns is an excellent stretch of road.

A log cabin built in 1828 is the oldest extant building in town, on Shake Rag Alley, formerly the heart of the Mineral Point business district. The former blacksmith shop is adjacent to the cabin; dating to 1836, it now a houses a tea room and antique store.

One of the elaborate miniature landscapes set up in the Toy Train Barn just outside of Argyle, Wisconsin on Highway 81.

The historic downtown streets are lined with small, delightfully quaint shops. No trip to Mineral Point would be complete without trying authentic Cornish pasties served at one of the many village restaurants.

Pendarvis House and several other Cornish stone cottages have been restored. Don't miss tours of the Pendarvis complex, where costumed guides take you back through the history of Mineral Point. Pendarvis is open from May through mid-October.

Another famous landmark is the zinc statue of a dog that originally watched over the Gundry & Gray department store. Both of the men were from Cornwall and kept the tradition of using animal statues to identify the stores.

Orchard Lawn, an eleven-acre estate surrounding the Gundry house, is now the property of the Mineral Point Historical Society; the house serves as a museum for artifacts from Mineral Point and Iowa County.

Tiny Pendarvis House is the oldest Cornish stone cottage in Mineral Point.

Other points of interest include The Opera House, which still serves as an entertainment focal point for the town. Movies, concerts, and performances by The Shake Rag Players are all still held in the beautiful building, which was designed by the architectural firm of Claud and Stark who designed the Orpheum Theatre.

Mineral Point also has the oldest surviving railroad depot in Wisconsin. Recently re-opened as the Mineral Point Railway Museum, the depot houses a unique collection of railroad artifacts from the town and surrounding area.

Several parks are available for those who wish to just stop and relax in a lovely outdoor setting. Watertower Park, Ted Galle Park, Jerusalem Park, Library Park, and Soldiers Memorial Park all provide places for a picnic lunch or a spot to enjoy a quiet break.

Just north of Mineral Point on Highway 23, the American Players Theatre mounts fine productions of classical theatre in a lovely outdoor setting with picnic areas and food available on the grounds.

The restoration work in Mineral Point is a continuous affair with more historic buildings being renovated into art studios, businesses, galleries, shops, and homes.

Highway 151 leads you down to Belmont, where you turn north on CTH G to get to First Capitol of Wisconsin State Park. This marks the site where the legislators from the Territory of Wisconsin met for forty-six days in 1836. The Council House Chambers are furnished with antiques from the period, and there is a museum in the Supreme Court Building.

For those feeling energetic, a climb to the top of the sixty-four-foot observation tower at nearby Belmont Mounds State Park will give you a wonderful panoramic view of three states.

Continuing west on G, you enter Platteville, the home of the campus of the University of Wisconsin, Platteville. Football fans will be interested to know that this is where the Chicago Bears used to hold their training camp each July. Platteville is also the home of the Rollo Jamison Museum where a guided tour takes you back in time to the turn of the 20th century. Many items that made up life in that era are on display.

There is also The Mining Museum, which includes a walk into the Bevans mine which once produced over two million pounds of lead in a year. You can visit a headframe, which shows how zinc ore was hoisted from the mine for hand sorting. The tour also includes a ride around the museum grounds in an ore car pulled by a 1931 locomotive. On the second floor of the mining museum building is the Roundtree Gallery, which exhibits works by area artists.

The biggest landmark, though, is the giant M— the world's largest—which students in the Mining

College cut into a mound overlooking the city, and both residents and visitors climb the M. Always impressive is the UW-P Homecoming Parade in October, climaxed by the lighting of the M.

The world's largest M is a famous landmark in Platteville. Students at the mining college cut the M into the mound.

A curvy ride down Highway 151 takes you to Dickeyville where you'll not want to miss the famous Grotto. Father Matthias Wernerus built the Grotto in the 1920s as a religious and patriotic shrine on the grounds of the Holy Ghost Catholic Church. The Grotto is only twenty-five feet high, thirty feet wide, and twenty-five feet deep, but stepping into the main cave will give you the feeling that you're standing in a huge structure. The colors and ornamentation are breathtaking and the religious and patriotic gardens are also colorful and unique. Very little of the mortar which holds the multicolored stones and pieces of glass together is visible.

The Catholic Church in Dickeyville is a must-stop.

At Dickeyville, you will connect with Highway 35, a route that figures often in our travels to the north. The first stop will be the connected towns of Tennyson and Potosi.

In the early 1800s Potosi, then known as Snake Hollow, was Wisconsin's largest city. Nestled between two sets of bluffs, the main street of the town seems to meander along for miles.

The Passage through Time Museum celebrates the history of the Potosi-Tennyson area. Included in the displays are Native American artifacts and exhibits on farming, mining, the Mississippi River, and the historic Potosi Brewery. There are also collections of World War II memorabilia, John Deere toy tractors, and historical records.

You might also enjoy a visit to the St. John Mine. A journey through the mine recreates the lives of "badgers," as the miners were called, who gave Wisconsin its nickname "The Badger State." A hiking trail leads to the badger huts, relics of where miners lived while digging lead from the mines.

Tennyson-Potosi is also known as the Catfish Capital of Wisconsin and the annual Catfish Festival is held during the second weekend in August.

The Point is a finger of land extending six-tenths of a mile into the Mississipp and is a wildlife refuge. This is a major stop for birds on the migration route; over 270 species have been sighted, including eagles, snow geese, American pelicans, and swans.

The Grant River Recreation Area overseen by the Army Corps of Engineers (COE), includes seventy-three campsites located on the Mississippi. This is an excellent campground that includes a shower house, an amenity not always available at COE parks. Many evenings around the campfire are enhanced by brilliantly colorful sunsets.

Even if you're not planning to camp, River Lane Road, which circles the twin towns, is worth a trip. This narrow, twisting, and challenging road covers only about five miles, but concentrated in that short distance is some marvelous scenery. The road ends on Routes 61 and 35, right beside a very welcome wayside rest area.

Taking Highway 61 north you reach Lancaster, scenically located on a ridge that is surrounded by lovely valleys and rocky bluffs. This "City of the Dome" is also the county seat. The glass and copper dome of the Courthouse dominates the landscape. Several monuments and memorials around town include the nation's first Civil War Memorial (1867). A stroll around the Courthouse will be a nice diversion as well as being educational. Inside the courthouse are many murals and a beautiful rotunda.

Two bikers stop for a rest at the Grant River Recreation Area. The bikes are a Harley 2003 Sportster and a KTM Adventure.

For history buffs having an interest in African-American culture and legends, an enlightening visit can be made to the Cunningham Museum. The Pleasant Ridge Cemetery marks the area of one of the first African-American settlements in Wisconsin.

If you are in need of a welcome break from the bikes, a stop at Shreiner Park gives you the opportunity to enjoy nature trails and use an exercise and jogging course. Here you can relax in a lovely valley enhanced by impressive rock outcroppings. Other parks with rest areas or picnic spots include Memorial Park and Ryland Park. Klondike Park, located two miles north of the town, is famous for its trout stream, or you might like to try your luck fishing in the Grant River.

Continuing up Route 61, you soon reach Fennimore where on weekends you can enjoy a ride on a miniature train while visiting the grounds of the Fennimore Railroad Museum. The Fennimore Doll and Toy Museum takes you back to childhood, with more than eighty display cases of antique toys.

Oakwood Nature Park allows you to explore a three-and-a-half mile hiking trail while observing a variety of birds, trees, and flowers native to the area. There are also more than one hundred miles of excellent trout streams within a ten-mile radius of the town.

After a short trip west on Highway 18, you can turn south on County Road K, just before the village of Mt. Ida. This road brings you back to Lancaster and a trip over to Beetown on Highway 81. Turning to the southeast you connect with CTH U back to Potosi, justifiably a favorite trek for motorcycle riders.

In Potosi you turn onto Highway 133, a section of the Great River Road. This takes you over to Cassville and a car ferry which transports you across the Mississippi and over into Iowa. However, a stop in Cassville will be worth your time. Just at the edge of town on CTH VV is the Nelson Dewey State Park. A drive through the winding roads of the park takes you to some spectacular overlooks of the Mississippi and the historical Stonefield Village located just across the road from the park entrance. Indian mounds are in evidence near the picnic areas and give a glimpse of the culture that flourished long before the white man settled in this part of the country. Some of the mounds are over 2000 years old.

The park was originally part of the estate of the first governor of Wisconsin, and many of the buildings and the stone fences remain from that period. A visit to the estate is coupled with a tour of Stonefield Village, a historical village of the 1800s which serves as an open-air museum; the State Agricultural Museum is located at the entrance. The village is open seven days a week from Memorial Day through Labor Day and on weekends into early October.

For a challenging ride, you might like to head up CTH VV, which twists along the base of heavily wooded bluffs. Be particularly alert for wildlife while traveling this road. A slight jog to the right on CTH V and then a left turn back onto VV brings you to CTH A. Turn left to head back toward the river and the small town of Bagley, known for its great fishing. Camping is available in Bagley at Jellystone Park. The road letter here changes to X and then goes up to the next fishing resort town of Wyalusing and to the marvelous Wyalusing State Park.

It is easy to see why Wyalusing was chosen as Wisconsin's first state park. The location is perfect, on the bluffs overlooking the confluence where the Wisconsin River flows into the Mississippi. Visitors can lose themselves in nature in the park's 2674 acres. The many Indian mounds dotting the top of the bluffs show that the earliest inhabitants also enjoyed the beauty of the area. For those interested in watching the stars, the Lawrence L. Huser Astronomy Center hosts programs twice a month by the Starsplitters of Wyalusing organization. Pads are available to set up your own telescope if you desire.

A full-time naturalist is on duty at the park and a nature interpretive center provides outdoor programs for the visitors. The park also includes 109 campsites, some with electrical hookups and some overlooking the Wisconsin River Valley. At dusk, you can watch the lights of Prairie du Chien begin to sparkle along the bank of the Mississippi. Back on CTH C our journey leaves the park and heads down to Highway 18 and the beginning of a side trip up the Wisconsin River.

A lookout point in Wyalusing State Park provides a spectacular view of the Wisconsin River as it flows into the Mississippi.

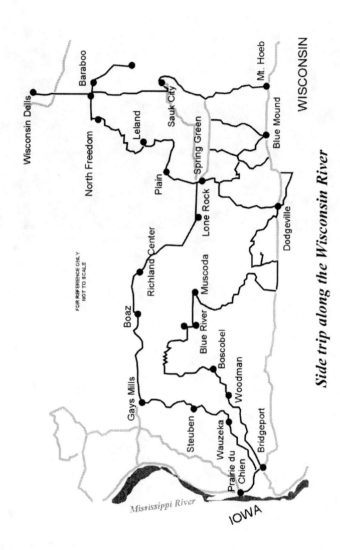

Side trip along the Wisconsin River

CHAPTER FOUR

RIDE THE LOWER WISCONSIN RIVER

A side trip along the Wisconsin River starting at the bridge on Highway 18 and heading east will include beautiful scenery, good food, and history at every turn. You can visit the summer home of Frank Lloyd Wright, the father of modern architecture, at Spring Green; see a large collection of priceless antique circus wagons at Baraboo; and head over to sample the carnival-like atmosphere of the Wisconsin Dells.

County Road C crosses Route 18 just before the bridge across the Wisconsin River. Remain on C, and you will follow close beside the river as you pass through and around several state conservation tracts. You will really enjoy the CTH C if you like twists, turns, and hills. For several miles the road is wedged between the backwaters of the Wisconsin River and the bottom of a series of bluffs.

When you reach Highway 133, a swing to the north takes you back to the river at Boscobel. The town's name comes from the French words *bosque belle*, or "beautiful woods," given to the area by the famous French explorers Louis Joliet and Jacques Marquette.

The Boscobel Hotel, built in 1865, has a unique claim to fame. Here, in 1898, two Christian traveling salesmen had the idea to form a Christian Travelers Association. From this small beginning the Gideon Society was created, and since then the group has placed millions of Bibles in lodging houses worldwide. The hotel now offers fine dining from Thursday through Sunday.

Other places of interest include the Boscobel Depot Museum that also houses the Chamber of Commerce office, the old schoolhouse, and Wisconsin's last remaining Grand Army of the Republic Hall where one hundred seventy-eight Civil War veterans are buried in the cemetery there. The first weekend in August Boscobel is the scene of one of the largest Civil War reenactments in the Midwest.

The town has six parks: Bluffview, Memorial, Northside, Scout Cabin, Westside, and Kronsage. This last park includes the public swimming pool and other sports facilities.

For another fun ride, cross the river at Boscobel and take Highway 61 north to CTH S. Turn east for a short but challenging trip enhanced by awesome scenery. Continue on S over to F, turn right and head down to Route 60. Turn left and go over to Port Arthur where you can cross the bridge to Blue River and reconnect with Highway 133.

This road continues to follow the river to Muscoda, located at the edge of Grant County, and Avoca, which lies just inside Iowa County. Near these two villages lies the nine hundred-acre Avoca Prairie, the largest tall grass prairie east of the Mississippi. In the days before the area was settled the tall grass prairie covered over two million acres, but now only about two thousand acres survive.

Avoca Lakeside Park surrounds a group of effigy mounds and also has 80 campsites.

Muscoda is known as the morel mushroom capital of Wisconsin. The Morel Mushroom Festival is held in the village the weekend after Mother's Day. The well known metal sculptor Ellis Nelson calls Muscoda home, and his work can be found around the village.

Take County Road G south out of Muscoda and then swing onto County Q. About four miles before you reach the village of Highland, stay alert for signs to the Spurgeon Vineyards and Winery.

The interesting tour of the facility includes grapevine pruning, the winemaking process, equipment operation, and the bottling line. Tours are held at noon each day, and don't overlook a visit to the wine-tasting room and gift shop. In October the winery hosts a harvest festival.

The Highland Village Park is an excellent place to stop for a break. There are fifteen acres of green space to enjoy, with four picnic shelters, grills, and picnic tables.

Turn south on County I for a trip down to Highway 18 and a turn east to the town of Montfort and its well-known wind farm. It is fascinating to watch acres of modern white windmill blades spinning as they steadily turn non-polluting wind into electrical power.

If you follow Highway 18, east, you will enter the village of Cobb, famous for its annual corn boil, held one weekend early in August. The actual date of the event depends on the timing of the harvest, but if you are lucky enough to hit the right weekend, you can enjoy some of the best sweet corn the area has to offer.

A few miles to the north of Cobb off Highway 80 you will find the beautiful 2000-acre Blackhawk Lake Recreation Area. The 220-acre lake provides opportunities for camping, swimming, hiking, boating, and fishing.

Continue north on Highway 80 to County Q and another scenic twisting ride back down to Highway 18 just west of Dodgeville.

There is much to see and do in the Dodgeville area so you might want to spend a day or two exploring. Luckily there are several excellent motels, bed and breakfasts, and restaurants in the town.

It definitely will be worth your time to stop at the Chamber Visitor's Center on Iowa Street and pick up information on the sights.

A visit to the Iowa County Historical Society also will be informative. The Society office is in the restored cabin built in 1827 by Henry Dodge, for whom the town is named. This is the oldest surviving building in Iowa County.

In 1859 the foundation was laid for the Iowa County Courthouse, which is now the oldest continuously-active courthouse in Wisconsin. Across the street, the Courthouse Inn restaurant displays a thirty-foot mural by local artist Jeb Prazak and offers a full-service menu of fine home-cooked food.

Dodgeville is the headquarters of the well-known clothing company, Land's End. Many bargains can be found at the Land's End Outlet Store in the historic downtown section. The Land's End Visitors Center at the corporate headquarters offers tours detailing the company's history.

A graceful row of the windmills dominates the landscape near Montfort, Wisconsin.

A six-mile trip to the east on County Road BB brings you to Folklore Village, an educational center which encourages you to learn about your ethnic heritage by keeping alive the folklore and customs from the varied settlers of the area. A large part of their mission is to connect the present generation to the traditions of their ancestors.

Just north of Dodgeville, the Governor Dodge State Park is the second largest and one of the busiest parks, in Wisconsin. Among the gorgeous attractions in the park are two lakes, a waterfall, beaches, bluffs, and valleys. In all there are 5200 scenic acres to explore.

Near the entrance to the park are Dolby Stables and Mineral Museum. The Museum hosts one of the largest collections of minerals found in the U.S. with unique minerals on display such as a 315-pound Brazilian agate, a 215-pound amethyst, and several other large specimens. Be sure to check out the lovely mosaic picture of "Man O' War" by artist Joe Phetteplace. After browsing through the gift shop, if you're inclined, you can mount up for a trail ride on the original off-road method of transportation.

Continuing north on Route 23, you find yourself once more back at the Wisconsin River just across from the town of Spring Green. County Highway C is a short but attention-keeping stretch of road, where you will find "Taliesin North," the summer home of famed architect Frank Lloyd Wright. A tour of the Frank Lloyd Wright Center will give you insight into the genius shown by the man who changed the world of architecture. The site offers several different guided tours of the 600-acre property. A short distance along CTH C, you come to Tower Hill State Park. You can climb to the smelter house and shot tower, where from 1833 to 1861 lead from all over Southwestern Wisconsin was brought to be formed into lead shot. The park includes an excellent campground.

The Frank Lloyd Wright Center at Taliesin North, the summer home of the father of modern architecture.

One more interesting stop along C is the famous House on the Rock. In 1945, Alex Jordan decided to take advantage of the wonderful views from the top of Deer Shelter Rock by building his dream home, and the House on the Rock has become one of the area's top attractions. The main house sits 400 feet above the valley floor; from every window the panoramic vistas are breathtaking.

Over the years, only the rock has remained the same, as new exhibits have continuously opened. You will be thrilled by visits to the Streets of Yesterday and the many rooms featuring an almost indescribable variety of collections. Don't miss the world's largest carousel and all of the organs and calliopes on display.

Those who enjoy classical theater in a casual setting will enjoy attending a performance of the American Players Theatre. This outdoor playhouse offers productions of Shakespeare, as well as that of works by more modern playwrights.

Take Highway 14 east and you soon come to Peck's Fruit Market, a great place to stop and refresh yourself with excellent produce. Further along on 14 you will find the village of Arena and the Arena Cheese Store, the home for lovers of fresh cheese curd. Many other varieties of cheese and meat products are also available.

If you now desire some more undeveloped surroundings, a trip on some of the county roads will be just what is needed. Return back a couple of miles on Highway 14 and turn onto County H south, to the hamlet of Hyde. Here a turn onto Mill Road will take you to Hyde's Mill. This lovely spot leaves no question as to why photographers are lured to the site.

This friendly mouse greets visitors to the Arena Cheese store, home of Co-jack cheese and delicious fresh curd.

The tranquil beauty of Hyde's Mill, one of the most photographed landmarks in Iowa County.

For those interested in the supernatural, the trip can continue down H to Ridgeway where you can attempt to search for the Ridgeway Phantom. This ghost traces back to one of two young men who was murdered at McKillip's Saloon in 1840. Many folks believe that the Phantom departed when the town burned in 1910, but others insist that he still roams the surrounding woods.

Following the foray into ghost hunting you turn east on Highway 18 or take CTH ID over to Barneveld. There you might like to drop down on CTH K south and enjoy some wine tasting at the Botham Vineyards and Winery.

Stay on CTH K south for a really fun road to ride with sweeping curves and great scenery. Stop at Hollendale and visit the lovely old estate built by Nick Englebert, an immigrant from the Austro-Hungarian Empire. The exterior of the farmhouse is decorated with concrete set with a colorful mosaic of stones and glass, and the grounds are adorned with concrete statuary and set with a variety of decorative materials.

Leaving Grandview, you can retrace your path up CTH K, which will give you a different perspective of the road, or you can take Highway 39 west to CTH F and up to Blue Mounds.

Once again on CTH K north, you go up to Blue Mound Road and a visit to Blue Mound State Park, the highest point in Southern Wisconsin. This park definitely should be added to your agenda and features two lookout towers which give spectacular views of the countryside. The park is open year round and has 78 camping sites.

Both roads K and Blue Mounds are excellent and beautiful roads. County Road K can also be accessed from Highway 14 just east of Arena. Another great side trip for bikers is County Road T which goes between Barneveld and Highway 23, and County Road Z which branches off T to the south. It is worth a bit of circling and backtracking to investigate all the exciting, breathtaking roads in this area. It helps to think that this is exploration and not being lost; that you are considering the road not taken, or the road less traveled, not one that has you hopelessly turned around and confused.

The concrete-covered façade of the Grandview farmhouse overlooks the concrete art displayed on the lawn.

Two other interesting destinations are located east along Highways 18 & 151. Just outside of Blue Mounds is Cave of the Mounds, a National Natural Landmark. The entrance to the cave was discovered when it was opened by a quarry blast in 1939, and inside the cave is a magnificent array of jewel-like stalagmites, stalactites, and underground pools of water.

A short trip up County Road F brings you to Brigham County Park and a chance to sit and enjoy the panoramic view of the Wisconsin River Valley. The park is named after Ebenezer Brigham, one of the first settlers to the area. There are also primitive campsites and picnic areas in the park.

Just off of Cave of the Mounds Road you can turn off onto CTH JG and head over to Little Norway, a re-created Norwegian settlement. The unusual buildings here include one with a traditional Norwegian sod roof and the Norway Building, which was displayed at the 1893 Chicago World's Fair. When the fair closed the building was moved to Lake Geneva, Wisconsin, until 1935 when it was permanently located in Little Norway.

A special package rate is available for those who visit both Cave of the Mounds and Little Norway on the same day.

Leaving Little Norway, turn left on County JG for a spectacular ride twisting among the high bluffs. This will bring you to at Stewart Park at the edge of Mt. Horeb. You just might want to stop and unwind here. After a short rest, head up the hill to Lake Street in Mt. Horeb.

The Norway House was Norway's exhibit at the 1893 Chicago World's Fair. It has been part of Little Norway since 1935.

In Mt. Horeb, don't miss the Mustard Museum, a shrine to the "king of condiments," which houses over four thousand two hundred jars, bottles, and tubes of mustard. You can earn a degree from Poupon U, visit the tasting table to sample hundreds of varieties, learn the history of mustard, or purchase anything mustard in the gift shop.

The greatest celebration is held on National Mustard Day, the first Saturday of August. Mustard fanciers paint the town yellow with everything from mustard games to mustard ice cream. You might also wish to go on a troll hunt, as you will find the diminutive characters lurking all along the main street.

From Mt. Horeb you can head north on Route 78 to Sauk City and Prairie du Sac, twin cities offering several lovely parks in which to stop and rest.

During the first weekend in September, Marion Park in Prairie du Sac is the scene of the Wisconsin State Cow Chip Throw. Beginning with the Cow Chip Challenge on Friday evening, the fun continues on Saturday with the Cow Chip Classic 10K run and fun activities throughout the day.

You can also visit the Wollersheim Winery, where a guided tour educates you in the process of winemaking and finishes with a wine tasting. You can choose from over a dozen different wines in the gift shop or visit the wine garden for a glass of wine and some fine Wisconsin cheese.

The first weekend in October marks the Grape Stomp Festival, which would make a fun stop on your trip. Think Lucille Ball here!

A beautiful drive up Highway 78 and then a turn onto the equally scenic Highway 133 will take you up to Devil's Lake State Park, one of the most popular in the state. You might want to spend some extra time exploring both the north and south shores. Other points of interest in the park include some effigy mounds built by the earliest inhabitants of the region and a swimming pool.

The fishing pier at the south shore picnic area on Devil's Lake gives a wonderful view of the surrounding bluffs.

Four miles due east of Devil's Lake is Parfrey's Glen, which has the distinction of being declared the state's first Natural Area. This is a fragile area, and visitors must stay on the paths and not disturb the natural surroundings in any way. A hiking trail follows a small creek to the upper end of the gorge.

Back on Highway 133, you continue north to Baraboo and Circus World Museum, a must stop for "children of all ages." This was the original winter home of Ringling Brothers' "The Greatest Show on Earth." A full history of the circus is presented at the museum, with daily performances under the big top. The outstanding feature of the museum is the world's largest collection of antique circus wagons, beautiful and ornate works of art which are breathtaking.

For several years these priceless and irreplaceable wagons were loaded onto a special circus train and transported across Southern Wisconsin to Milwaukee for the annual Circus Day Parade. There teams of draft horses from throughout the Midwest assembled to pull the wagons through the downtown parade route. In 2004 the Circus Parade returned to its home in Baraboo. No matter where it is located, the parade's loyal following gather for the event held on the Fourth of July weekend.

Highway 12 out of West Baraboo takes you north to the Wisconsin Dells, the major tourist area of Southern Wisconsin. You can enjoy boat tours to the fantastic upper and lower Dells, have an exciting ride on the Ducks; take a horse-drawn wagon ride through Lost Canyon; or spend days visiting the numerous shops, water parks, amusement parks, arcades, restaurants, and tourist attractions which abound in the area.

If you are exhausted after sampling the delights of the Dells, a couple of quiet places to recoup are Mirror Lake and Rocky Arbor State Parks, both of which are nearby.

Mirror Lake receives its name from its calm surface, which reflects its surroundings with the clarity of a mirror. This is an excellent park for tent campers, and there is also fishing, swimming, and hiking in the park.

The two hundred thirty-one acres of Rocky Arbor State Park are famous for its unique rock formations. The picturesque walls of the Rocky Arbor Gorge have been fashioned out of sandstone, and geologists place the age of the gorge at five hundred million years.

One of the priceless circus wagons on display at Circus World Museum in Baraboo.

From Mirror Lake, swing over to Route 12 and go south to West Baraboo where you can catch Highway 136 to CTH PF. This will bring you down to North Freedom and the Steam Passenger Train operated by Mid-Continent Railway.

A four-mile scenic trip by rail takes you to La Rue and Quartzite Lake. The train runs four times a day from mid-May to Labor Day; it also makes autumn weekend color trips during October.

Returning to PF, you can then follow the scenic trail down to CTH C at Leland and over to Natural Bridge State Park. To see the Natural Bridge, you have to leave the bikes and hike to the landmark. Turn back right on CTH C and follow it to B where a right turn will take you to Plain, located in the heart of the dairy country.

A visit to the Cedar Grove Cheese Factory will allow you to view cheese making.

Another stop should be the lovely St. Luke's Catholic Church. This Romanesque building, overlooking the village, is one of the largest and most beautiful in Southwestern Wisconsin. The Italian marble altars and the stained glass windows are truly wonderful. Behind the church a pathway, lined with the Stations of the Cross, leads to the sixty-year-old St. Anne's Shrine. A few steps further you will find a replica of the Lourdes Grotto set in the hill.

Following Route 23 south, you come to the town of Spring Green. You can spend a day browsing the art galleries and specialty shops in the village and surrounding area. During the last full weekend in June, over two hundred artists line the downtown streets during the Spring Green Arts and Crafts Fair.

As you head west along Highway 60 a tall spire of sandstone appears. This has long been a landmark for those traveling the river, and it gives the hamlet of Lone Rock its name. The town has one more claim to fame: On January 30th, 1951 the town recorded a temperature of minus fifty-three degrees, earning the title of the coldest spot in the nation.

Highway 14 will take you northwest to Richland Center, the birthplace of Frank Lloyd Wright. During World War I, Wright designed a warehouse for food wholesaler A. D. German. Often called the Mayan temple for its unusual concrete frieze around the top floor and for the narrow window, this is the only building designed by Wright in that era that remains standing.

The Red Door Gallery in Richland Center exhibits the work of the many talented local artists and crafters. Another interesting spot is the footbridge across the Pine River. This cable suspension bridge and boardwalk hangs only a few feet above the river and marshes.

Krouskop Park, on the northwest side of the city, is the scene of the largest country music festival in Southwestern Wisconsin. Star Spangled Celebration features three days of top Nashville acts and quality local entertainers. The event is held during the first full weekend in June

The beauty of the area is celebrated with the Center Color Fiesta during the first full weekend of October. On Saturday evening, following a delicious spaghetti supper, the "Canyon of Lights" parade is held.

When visiting anywhere in Wisconsin during the height of the fall color season, it is wise to make advance reservations, as lodging is at a premium. Often it is impossible to find a room, despite the many hotels and motels throughout the state.

Continuing west on Highway 14 for about nine miles you reach Highway 171 at Boaz, where in 1897 four young brothers, who were checking a flood gate after a severe storm, noticed that some huge bones had been uncovered on the bank of the creek. The find proved to be the first known mastodon bones to be discovered in Wisconsin. The Boaz Mastodon now resides in the Geology Museum at the University of Wisconsin in Madison. A historical marker designating the site of the discovery can be found along Highway 14 a mile east of Boaz.

Highway 171 continues to take you west toward Gays Mills, where a ridge ride takes you through the most concentrated line-up of apple orchards in the Tri-State area.

On Mother's Day Weekend, the town holds the Annual Spring Festival, and the miles of apple trees in bloom are a marvelous sight to behold. The apple harvest begins in August and continues through mid-October. Here you can find almost every known variety of apples.

The Annual Gays Mills Apple Festival is held during the last full weekend in September. Each orchard has its own ambiance, and you will also find plums, cherries, grapes, squash, pumpkin, and other produce during the season. Many of the orchard markets also offer fresh, mouth-watering bakery goods.

A brightly-colored wagon marks the parking lot to one of the many orchards near Gays Mills.

Other attractions in Gays Mills are Pioneer Log Cabin Village and the Museum of the Kickapoo.

Looking south from the apple orchard road you get a spectacular view of the Kickapoo River Valley. The Kickapoo River covers only thirty-three miles as the crow flies, but it twists its way through the Kickapoo Valley for one hundred miles (as the fish swims), one of the most crooked rivers in the world. Highway 133 follows the bends of the Kickapoo as it heads south from Gay's Mills.

The Kickapoo Valley is spectacular when seen from the overlook in Husher County Park just north of Wazeka.

At the mouth of the Kickapoo River, you will find the small village of Wazeka. Those interested in the life of the earliest inhabitants must stop at the Kickapoo Indian Caverns. The prehistoric Indians found shelter in the many rooms of this onyx cave. A museum filled with artifacts explains the early lifestyles of the hunters and gatherers. The caverns are open from May 15th through October 31st. The road to the caverns is a nice winding ride but be aware that the actual driveway to the caverns is a gravel washboard that goes straight up.

You can find out more about the history of the area at the Lower Wisconsin River Genealogical and Historical Research Center. Wazeka also boasts Century Hall, a restored theater and community center.

The side trip up the lovely Wisconsin River ends with a trip on Route 60 to the town of Prairie du Chien.

The sign at the head of the path beckons visitors to explore the Kickapoo Caverns, just outside of Wazeka.

Wisconsin Route 35 north

CHAPTER FIVE

PRAIRIE DU CHIEN NORTH

Wisconsin Route 35 north out of Prairie du Chien gives one the feeling of riding along a coastline as the road is sandwiched between the river and high bluffs, and many people think this area outshines the Hudson River Valley in New York. Along the way, side trips will take you into ethnic settlements and through a large Amish territory. Be sure to watch out for horses and buggies as you bend around curves and top the hills. For those seeking a challenging ride, this chapter will also introduce you to the Midwest's answer to Deal's Gap.

Long before the white man came to the prairie, this area was a neutral ground, where Indians met to barter. Since then it ,has been a major depot for the fur trade and a military outpost, where Black Hawk surrendered and was imprisoned.

The first white men to see the beautiful area were the Marquette and Joliet party in 1673, when the land was claimed for France. Nicholas Perrot established a fur depot in 1680, and the first white settlers arrived in the 1770s.

The town was named after the Indian chief Alim, which meant dog in English. When the French arrived, they named the settlement Prairie du Chien, or Prairie of the Dog. After the Revolutionary War, the area was included in the Northwest Territory and ceded to the new republic.

The first Crawford County Courthouse was built here in 1835; the present courthouse was built on the same site in 1867. Genealogical help is available at the deeds office from 10:00 a.m. to 4:00 p.m. daily.

The old Territorial Prison is located beneath the Crawford County Courthouse and tours are provided by appointment. If you decide to visit "The Dungeon," as it is called, you will be happy that you were not a felon in the early days. There was only one way in and one way out of the prison, and that was through the door opening on Beaumont Road. The five cells which contain bunk beds seven feet long, five feet wide, and seven feet tall; the only light is from the tiny windows on the north which are too small to allow a man to escape. The heavy iron doors make it almost impossible to see out.

Two smaller cells only three feet wide were used to hold miscreants for a shorter period of time, and the solitary confinement cells are barely tall enough for a person to stand. Leg irons and arm chains completed the security arrangements. The ceiling in the north cellblock is heavy steel.

At the other end of the spectrum a visit to Villa Louis will acquaint you with the country estate of the Dousman family who rose to prominence during the last days of the upper Mississippi Valley fur trade. The family also invested in timber, railroads, steamship companies, and farmland and became one of the wealthiest families in the new territories.

Restored fur-trading fort on the grounds of Villa Louis in Prairie du Chien, Wisconsin. The mansion and grounds of Villa Louis have been restored to their original splendor and are open to the public.

Villa Louis, the mansion home of the wealthy Dousman family in Prairie du Chien.

On Father's Day the Prairie Villa Rendezvous is held, one of the largest trade re-enactments in the Midwest. Over 400 lodges are erected, and craftsmen demonstrate the old crafts. If you get hungry strolling through the site, you can enjoy grilled buffalo burger, fry bread, Indian tacos, root beer, or sarsaparilla.

Other historic sites you might enjoy visiting are the Ft. Crawford Museum, which displays much history of the area, and St. Gabriel's Catholic Church, the oldest church in Wisconsin and the first built by Father Mazzuchelli. The tomb of Father Galtier, the founder of St. Paul, Minnesota, is located on the church grounds.

Leaving Prairie du Chien the drive up Highway 35 has been compared to the drive along the Rhine and reportedly outshines a trip up the Hudson River.

Along the road the bluffs seem to rise higher and the river seems to widen as you approach Lynxville. Here at Lock and Dam 9 you can often watch barges and riverboats lock through from scenic overlooks. The world's largest cigar store Indian also calls Lynxville home.

The lovely river vistas continue up to Ferryville where you can catch CTH C and head over to Soldier's Grove.

This town will be particularly fascinating to those with an interest in alternative energy, since Soldier's Grove was America's first solar village. Many of the buildings were designed to exploit the nonpolluting power of the sun.

Another excellent road north out of Prairie du Chien is Highway 27 which takes you further inland and up to the town of Mt. Sterling. Award-winning goat cheese is available at the Mt. Sterling Cheese Co-op. A short jaunt on up Highway 27 brings you to the intersection with CTH C where you can turn to either Soldier's Grove or Ferryville.

Highway 61 north out of Soldiers Grove will take you to Readstown in the heart of the Kickapoo Valley. Included among its three historic cemeteries is one for veterans of the Civil War. There is also an excellent park on the banks of the Kickapoo River.

Follow the twisting Kickapoo eight miles further upstream and you will come to the village of Viola. This is the home of the unique Horse and Colt Show held at the end of September, when the focus is on all things horse. From buggy rides to horse pulls to a wonderful horse parade, this will take you back to a more leisurely time.

Seven miles north of Viola is the village of LaFarge, the gateway to the 9000-acre Kickapoo Reserve, which allows unlimited opportunities for those who enjoy getting back to nature.

Take Route 82 heading northeast out of Lafarge over to where is joins Highway 33 and then continue on to the village of Hillsboro, the Czech Capital of Wisconsin.

Cesky Den (Czech Day) celebrates the heritage of the town. Ethnic dance, music, crafts, storytelling, and a Polka Mass are some of the featured activities at this festival held during the second weekend in June. The Historical Society in City Park maintains the Hillsboro Museum and Log Cabin.

A settlement once called Cheyenne Valley is nearby. This was the home of "Free Men of Color," and the population was made up of Blacks and Native Americans. These people and their descendents were successful farmers and members of the community. Alga Shivers, a second generation resident, built many of the famous round barns which still can be seen in the countryside around Hillsboro. Recently the Cheyenne Valley Heritage Society has been formed to preserve the settlement's history.

Hillsboro marks the eastern edge of Wisconsin's largest Amish community, which includes several area towns. This is a prime area in which to shop for unique and handcrafted items. Roadside signs will lead you to the many fine products and homemade foods that are produced. While visiting the Amish stores, please leave your cameras on the bikes. Taking pictures is tempting, but Amish beliefs prohibit them from having their pictures taken, and they appreciate having respect shown for their culture which includes no Sunday sales.

Turn back on 82 heading west out of Hillsboro and continue to CTH P, about six miles. A right turn takes you through the countryside to where CTH P joins Highway 131 south for a few miles before branching off west once more. Stay on P to Route 27 just outside of Westby. This stretch, about 26 miles of road, is full of sharp twists and will give you a real workout.

Westby is another town celebrating its Norwegian heritage and is called "A Little City with a Big Velkommen." Westby's *Syttende Mai* celebration honors Norway's Constitution Day, and is held yearly during the closest weekend to May 17.

Other points of interest in Westby include Coon Prairie Church, the twin spires have graced the village since 1909 and have been on the National Historic Registry since 1989. The history of the area can be found at the Thorsen House Museum. For luxurious accommodations try the Westby House Victorian Inn and Restaurant, you will enjoy elegant atmosphere and wake to a gourmet breakfast. Another great stop for food is the Westby Cooperative Creamery and indulge in some of their excellent cheeses and curd. Then head up Highway 14, stopping at the wayside to view Three Chimney Rock.

Coon Valley, ten miles up Highways 14 & 61, is also a center of Norwegian culture and history.

Skumsrud Heritage Farm is located one mile west of Coon Valley on 14/61. Here you can try your hand at ethnic and pioneer crafts such as rosemaling, knitting and woodcarving. This is also an open-air museum where you can visit eleven historic buildings including the Skumsrud Cabin built in 1853. The farm is operated by Norskedalen and is open daily from Memorial Day through Labor Day.

Norskedalen Nature and Heritage Center includes a modern visitors center, museums, gift shop, library, a pioneer farmstead, and hiking trails all nestled on 400 acres three miles north on CTH PI.

A mile east on Highways 14 & 61 brings you to CTH B and a trip south to Viroqua, a hamlet which has been rated as small town America at its best by *Reader's Digest, Smithsonian Magazine*, and *The Wall Street Journal*, and, of course, its residents.

Lovers of bluegrass music gather in July for the Viroqua Bluegrass Festival when musicians playing traditional instruments entertain with old fashioned bluegrass and gospel tunes.

The farmer's market on Main Street is a large one with a delightfully appealing variety of produce and Amish crafts. You can enjoy live entertainment at the Historic Temple Theatre. Or simply take a walking tour of the many historic sites in the town.

In mid August you can return to the color and excitement of the frontier with the town's annual Wild West Days. Stagecoach rides, gunfights, saloon brawls, and dance hall girls are all in evidence at during the three-day celebration.

South of Viroqua, CTH NN branches off to the west and then connects with N south to Highway 82. This takes you over to 27 South and then CTH B at Rising Sun and back west to the Great River Road.

Several small communities dot the banks of the river as you head north. Be sure to check out the fantastic view from the lookout point high above the river just north of Genoa.

Jim Rodewald of Milwaukee and Linda Kolander of Muskego take a break to admire the view from the lookout point near Genoa.

When you come down from the lookout point, instead of getting back on 35, turn left and follow the serpentine Spring Coulee Road up to CTH K. Turn left again and head over to CTH D for a nice ride to Stoddard.

Turn east on 162 at Stoddard and travel over to Chaseburg. A converted stone schoolhouse and several restored log cabins are downtown. You also can visit the Heartland Tradesman's Museum. A short trip back on 162 brings you to CTH K and a scenic ride northwest back to the Mississippi.

Highway 35 continues its scenic way along the Mississippi, giving you an ever-changing panorama of bluffs and boat traffic. The route passes through several small villages until reaching the city of LaCrosse.

European pioneers pushing west were awed by the increasing height of the bluffs and narrow valleys, which the French settlers called coulees. When they reached the 500-foot bluffs overlooking the Mississippi, they saw a group of Indians playing a game similar to the French game of LaCrosse and the town had found its name. In a short time the Prairie LaCrosse had become a major trading center for the area.

Today, LaCrosse the town and LaCrosse County remain popular gathering places. During your time in LaCrosse, you can enjoy a cruise on the Mississippi on your choice of riverboat rides.

The Julia Belle Swain and the LaCrosse Queen will take you back to gentler times when the paddlewheelers traversed the rivers. For a more modern outing, the Island Girl is a sleek one hundred fifty-passenger cruising yacht.

Another interesting prospect is the City Brewery Tour. The gift shop and the hospitality center where you can sample the brews are popular destinations.

One of the most scenic views in Wisconsin is found at Granddad's Bluff where you can enjoy seeing the city of LaCrosse and a three state view from this 600-foot lookout point. Head east on Main Street until it turns into Bliss Road as it begins its climb to the top of the bluff.

Many other fine museums and historic sites are open to the public. Victorian style is represented in the Hixon House, the ornate home of a local lumber baron. A Turkish nook makes this home unique among historic homes. The history of the Mississippi and its importance to the area is explained at the Riverside Museum. The history of LaCrosse from pre-historic times to the present day is explored at the Swarthout Museum.

Evening often brings a gorgeous sunset over Lake Onalaska.

LaCrosse also is home to several art galleries and venues for live entertainment. Lodging is readily available, as is a variety of eating preferences ranging from fine dining and ethnic fare to fast food outlets.

The Deke Slayton Airfest in June honors the history of flight and pays tribute to the pioneer astronaut who was a native to the area.

Adjacent to LaCrosse to the north is the town of Onalaska. Situated on a ridge above Lake Onalaska, this town offers wonderful views of the lake, islands, river, and the Minnesota Bluffs in the distance.

Of particular interest to motorcyclists is the annual Thunder Ride to Cure Diabetes in July. Riders can register and leave from LaCrosse Area Harley Davidson, Two Brothers Honda, or Steiger Power Sports.

A fun time also will be had at the Onalaska Sunfish Days in May. Held at the Onalaska Omni-Center and Van Riper Park the celebration offers something for all ages.

Highway 16 out of LaCrosse heading east follows the LaCrosse River over to West Salem, which boasts several historic homes, including the Palmer-Gullickson octagon house built by Dr. Horace Palmer in 1856 and originally located in nearby Neshonoc. When the railroad went through West Salem, the home was moved to that town.

Sunny the sunfish greets visitors to the town of Onalaska and to beautiful Lake Onalaska.

Other historic homes in West Salem are the Hamlin Garland Homestead, home of Pulitzer Prize winning author Hamlin Garland; and the home of Thomas Leonard, the founder of West Salem. In early June the city hosts the Dairy Days Celebration.

Experienced riders may want to take a small loop tour out of West Salem by heading up Highway 108. A series of sharp turns will keep you on your toes, because it is difficult not to be distracted by the eye-popping scenery. This road is said to rival "The Tail of the Dragon" at Deal's Gap in the Blue Ridge Mountains.

The route leads through Mindoro, where in mid-September the Spanferkel Celebration by the Mindoro Lions Club features some of the best roast pork you will ever taste. Spanferkel is a German word for pig.

If you continue up 108 to Melrose you will find two parks where you can stop for some much needed R&R before taking off again. You can go down 108 and hit 71 just south of Melrose and then go over to 162 south, or a bit further down you can pick up CTH C south for a slightly different view of the territory. Finally, you can face another pass down 108, this time from the north.

Any of these three routes will take you south to Highway 16 where you can head over to Sparta.

The history of transportation is displayed at the Deke Slayton Memorial Space and Bike Museum in Sparta. Exhibits range from the earliest bicycles through the dawn of aviation and continue on to the exploration of space.

Located at the junction of Routes 16 and 21, Sparta is also the home of the world's largest bicycle. The 30 foot high-wheeler was built in Sparta by the F.A.S.T. (Fiberglass Animals Shapes & Trademarks) Corporation.

The Monroe County Museum traces the history of Monroe County from pioneer times to the present.

Butterfest celebrates the dairy industry and is held during the second weekend in June. Featured attractions during the festival include a carnival, car show, quilt show, flea market, and a milking contest.

Add lots of food, a Sunday parade, live entertainment, and the Miss Sparta Pageant, and it all adds up to something for everyone to enjoy.

"Big Ben" rides the world's largest bicycle at the park in Sparta WI.

A trip down Highway 27 will take you to Route 33 where you can head east over to Cashton. For a breathtaking view head up to the top of St. Mary's Ridge and a visit to St. Mary's Church built over one hundred years ago. You can also book a tour of Amish country, with one stop including an Amish shop with locally made crafts and goodies.

Continue east on 33 to Ontario and the western entrance to Wildcat Mountain State Park. The park has a resident naturalist who will be happy to acquaint you with the rare plants and animals and the spectacular geology of this unique place.

For a different type of farm tour you might enjoy a visit to Kinney Valley Alpacas. The farm is open for tours year round and offers the opportunity to get up close and personal with these friendly and gentle creatures.

The first weekend in August you might want to head north to the town of Wilton for the Wilton Wood Turtle Days. A drive to Wilton on summer Sunday mornings is worthwhile, when a pancake breakfast is served by the Wilton Lions Club in the Wilton Village Park Campground. Or you can head east out of Ontario on CTH P to the village of Kendall, known as the polka capital of Monroe County. Kendall is also a stop on the famous Elroy-Sparta bicycle trail, and although motorcycles are not allowed on the trail, the county highways offer wonderful rides for our kind of bikers.

One of those rides is CTH W north from Kendall to A. Turn left onto A and over to N which will continue the northward trip to Highway 12/16 where another left turn will take you over to Tomah.

In late June, Tomah hosts the Wisconsin Dairyland National Tractor/Truck Pull, which is rated number one in the U.S. Entrants come from all over the country to compete in this noisy yet exciting event.

Each August the citizens of Tomah pay tribute to native son cartoonist Frank King who created the "Gasoline Alley" comic strip, basing many of the characters on Tomah residents. The actual "Gasoline Alley" is Tomah's Superior Avenue. The famous comic strip was created in 1915 and continues to be published today.

The Tomah Area Historical Society Museum gives the history of the town and surrounding countryside. You might also want to stop by Gillett Park and visit "The Little Red Schoolhouse." This authentic one room schoolhouse gives you a glimpse of the way education was handled in earlier times.

What would the Thanksgiving turkey be with out a cranberry side dish? Massachusetts is known for its cranberry bogs, but the cranberry marshes of Wisconsin are equally impressive. Tomah marks the gateway to Cranberry Country where you can visit the Cranberry Museum and gift shop and sample many products made with cranberries. In the Fall the huge cranberry marshes provide a colorful sea of red to complement the backdrop of fall colors. The Cranberry Festival is held in late September.

Heading southeast out of Tomah on Highway 12 you will come to Mill Bluff State Park just outside of the town of Camp Douglas. Here nature has sculpted several striking rock formations, and climbing the path and steps to the top of the bluff will give you a fantastic view. There is also a swimming pond with a nice sand beach. The park is part of the Ice Age National Scientific Reserve.

Camp Douglas is also the home to two combined military installations. Volk Field is a readiness-training complex operated by Air National Guard. Camp Williams belongs to the Army National Guard.

A restored 1896 log lodge on the grounds houses the Wisconsin National Guard Memorial Library and Museum, an appealing stop for those with an interest in military history.

CTH H leads out of Camp Douglas south to the small community of Hustler where you should make a left turn on to A toward New Lisbon. About halfway between the two towns you will pass between the twin bluffs. Although on private land these rocks contain some of the oldest and best preserved Indian petroglyphs in the state.

In New Lisbon you will learn about the earliest inhabitants of the region at Indian Mounds Park which preserves a group of effigy mounds including one of a long-tailed running panther, unique to the area since all other known panther effigies have straight legs. More Indian history and artifacts are available at the New Lisbon Memorial Library.

Take CTH M north out of New Lisbon to Highway 21. If you wish to get back to nature and view a wide variety of wildlife you might want to turn east toward Nacedah, while 43,656 acres of wetlands, known as the Great Central Wisconsin Swamp, now form the Nacedah National Wildlife Refuge. Interpretive programs and special events will give you an understanding of this unspoiled region that is essential for preserving the bio-diversity of the area.

Adjoining the refuge to the west is the 60,000-acre Central Wisconsin Conservation Area, and CTH H will take you through this area to the town of Mather. This is a prime hunting area for upland birds and waterfowl during the season. If you wish to camp in the area, it is necessary to get permission from the Meadow Valley Ranger Station.

Take CTH EE out of Mather where you can turn left onto E or turn right onto HH. Either road will bring you to Warrens and the heart of "Cranberry Country." Going down to E is the shorter route, but if you opt for the longer trip on HH you will turn south on O to get to Warrens.

The annual cranberry harvest totals over 2500 acres. Warrens also claims a second unusual export, sphagnum moss, prized by horticulturists for keeping plants and nursery stock alive. Wisconsin is the only place in the U.S. that commercially produces this product.

The Cranberry Festival held at the end of September is a major draw for visitors and includes tours of the cranberry marshes, browsing among the booths of over 1200 vendors, good food, and music, and of course, cranberries bring huge crowds to the area.

The country's only museum dedicated to the cranberry, the Wisconsin Cranberry Discovery Center, gives insight into the cranberry industry. When visiting the gift shop you can try some cranberry ice cream.

A colorful trip to watch a cranberry harvest is held the first Saturday in October at Wetherby Cranberry Marsh.

A sixty-five-site modern campground is located at McMullen County Park, or you can opt to stop for rest and lunch in the picnic shelter. You can also stretch your legs by hiking on the nature trail.

Continue south on O to Highway 12 and take it down to Route 21. Turn west for a trip over to Ft. McCoy which has been in operation since 1909. During WWII it served as a training post and prisoner of war camp. Today it functions as a total force war fighter-training center. Every year over 120,000 trainees pass through the camp, and a self-guided driving tour through the fort is available.

Camping and swimming are available at the Pine View Recreation Area and winter activities are highlighted at Whitetail Ridge Recreation Area.

Northwest of Ft. McCoy is the village of Cataract. Follow Highway 21 out of Ft. McCoy to CTH I at Angelo to visit this interesting area.

There are several "don't miss" sites in Cataract including the Wegner Grotto, The Little Falls Railroad and Doll Museum, and The Monroe County Local History Room Museum and Library.

Centerpiece of the Wegner Grotto is a small chapel constructed out of concrete, broken glass and pottery shards. Known locally as "The Little Glass Church," it was built around 1930 by Paul and Matilda Wegner. Other works of art at the Grotto include animals, a peace star, and a replica of the ship "Bremen." The Grotto is easily accessible from Highway 27.

For those interested in historical research, the Monroe County Local History Room Museum and Library houses archives about the history of the area.

Interesting exhibits take you from pioneer times to today's farming industry and also feature a look into the daily life on the frontier.

Two miles east of Cataract on CTH II is the Little Falls Railroad and Doll Museum which displays hundreds of dolls ranging in age from the 1800s to a collection of modern Barbies.

Three operating model railroad setups are in the railroad section of the museum. The history of railroading is introduced through books, videos, photos, and railroad art, and for youngsters there is an outdoor train ride.

Each weekend after Labor Day the Cataract Sportsmen's Club holds field days when locals and visitors alike enjoy shooting games, archery, trap and skeet shoots, music, food, and much more.

From Cataract you head for Holmen via Highway 27 south to the junction of Route 71 and turn right on 71 for a short jog over to 162. Turn south down to CTH T over to Mindoro where you can catch CTH D over to Holmen.

Holmen is located just north of LaCrosse along Highway 35 and this brings you back to the Mississippi. A newly-built, state-of-the-art aquatic center featuring 12,000 square feet of water is located beside Deer Wood Park. In August, the village holds its annual Kornfest.

Leaving Holmen, Route 35 takes you upriver into Trempealeau County, the southern frontier of Wisconsin's Indian Head Territory.

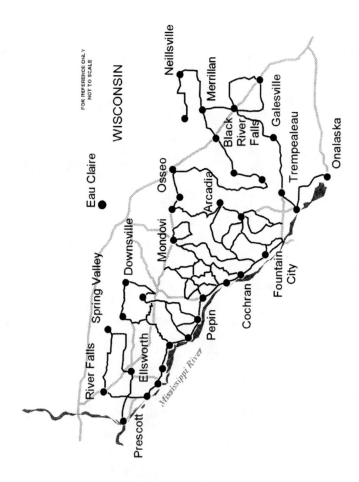

Continuing along scenic Route 35

CHAPTER SIX

THE NORTH COUNTRY

The wonderful ride along the river on Wisconsin's Route 35 will inspire you as you explore small villages, visit a mountain that seems to grow out of the water, browse a famous art fair, perhaps join in one of the large motorcycle flood runs, or just marvel at the gorgeous scenery. Leaving the river, you will encounter the peace and solitude of the north woods, visit a national memorial to Native American servicemen, and stop in Osseo for lunch at the finest ethnic restaurant in Wisconsin.

The name Trempealeau means "Mountain Soaking in Water," referring to the mountain located in the bay at Perrot State Park just north of the village. The view from the top of the bluff is breathtaking. The Trempealeau National Wildlife Refuge is close by the park.

The main street of Trempealeau has been listed on the National Register of Historic Places since 1984.

The Trempealeau hotel, restaurant, and saloon were built in 1871 and are popular places to stop.

Trempealeau Mountain stands by itself, surrounded by water, at Perrot State Park.

Lock and Dam 6 is located near downtown and has an observation tower where you can watch the boats and barges lock through and enjoy great views of the Mississippi and its islands.

During the weekend after July Fourth, the town holds its Annual Catfish Days.

Trempealeau County has laid out three audio loop tours for cars but some of these can also provide spectacular rides for motorcyclists.

Take CTH K northeast out of Trempeleau towards Galesville, although you might want to cut off onto CTH M and pass the only remaining round barn in the county, a unique structure made from poured concrete and located on private land.

Reconnecting with K you will arrive in Galesville, a small town nestled between rolling hills and centered by the lovely Lake Marinuka, named after Princess Marie Nounko, a granddaughter of legendary Chief Decorah. The grave of the princess is at the north end of the lake at Artic Springs.

In 1886 the beauty and fertility of Galesville inspired Rev. D. O. Van Slyke to write a book claiming that the area fit the Biblical description of the Garden of Eden. A statue of the Rev. Van Slyke, by artist Elmer Peterson, welcomes visitors to town.

Among the places to visit in the town are the Arnold House, Cance Home, Clark House Bed & Breakfast, and the Gale College Historic Site.

The Brush Trophy Room Museum displays over 250 mounted exotic animals. This is the largest bow-hunting trophy room in the world.

A swinging bridge crosses Beaver Creek and takes you to the hiking trails of Highland Park. Several other parks nearby also invite riders to stop for a rest.

A pleasant walkway will take you through the McGilvray bottoms and several one hundred-year-old drawstring bridges can be seen on McGilvray road.

The first Saturday in October the town hosts the Apple Affair. Be prepared for a treat to the senses when you first encounter the aroma from the ten-foot apple pie that takes over the downtown square. To make sure you don't go hungry there is also the omelet breakfast and the brat lunch.

Highway 54 east out of Galesville will take you over to Black River Falls.

Getting back to nature is easy at Black River Falls. First there is the adjacent Black River Falls State Forrest. Then you can try scuba diving nearby at Wazee Lake, a former mining site that is now the deepest freshwater lake in Wisconsin.

You can meet beautiful maidens, strolling minstrels, skilled craftsmen and gallant knights during the third weekend in June at the Black River Falls Medieval Faire. This is held at the NCN North, LLC Campground.

The fourth weekend of June is the Black River Rumble, also held at NCN North. This motorcycle rally includes bands, a poker run, and a fun time for all.

The Karner Blue Butterfly Festival, held on the second Saturday in July, brings to attention the tiny, endangered, Karner Blue Butterfly. A turn-of-the-century trolley ride will take you to the butterfly habitat. While in the town, you can enjoy good food and browsing the many vendors' booths.

One more chance to step back in time can be found at The Merchant General Store built in 1912 and maintaining the old fashioned look of the interior. A potbelly stove with an inviting checkerboard set up alongside occupies one corner, and an old fashioned cash register is still in use.

Another popular spot is the Pioneer Brewery, established in 1856 by Ulrick Oderbolz and the first brewery in Wisconsin. It remained in business until prohibition shut it down. The site went through several different metamorphoses until it was re-opened as a modern state-of-the-art brewery in 1997. The company now produces Pioneer Lager and Pioneer Pale Ale.

A nice circle ride will take you south on Highway 12 to CTH O where a left turn onto O at Shamrock will take you past I-94 at Millston. Turn left onto Settlement Road and you will find a lovely ride through the Black River State Forest. Turn back to the left once more and you will return to Black River Falls.

A couple of miles north on Highway 12 & 27 brings you to CTH E and a ride over to Hatfield. Hatfield is the gateway to lovely Lake Arbutus. The town offers

spots at which to rest, picnic, and swim. Its location in
the Black River State Forest makes it a great place to
enjoy nature and view wildlife.

Take CTH I north out of Hatfield and then turn
right on to Route 95 and head over to Neilsville. There
"Chatty Belle," the world's largest talking cow, will
greet you. Alongside "Chatty Belle" you'll find the
world's largest cheese replica.

You will also definitely want to visit their
Highground Veterans Memorial. Originally conceived in
1965 to honor the memory of a fallen serviceman in
Vietnam it has grown into a tribute for all veterans. The
Highground has many unique features including being
home to the National Native American Vietnam Veterans
Memorial and The Earthen Dove Effigy Mound, a replica
of an early Native American mound. A popular
Highground Benefit Motorcycle Rally is held in August.

Turning west on Highway 10 you will head over
to CTH B, which will take you over to Highways 12 &
27. Turn south and continue down to the town of
Merrillan.

Merrillan is a lovely burg at which to stop for a
break. The downtown area features a beautiful waterfall
and one mile southeast of town you will find Oakwood
Lake, Trow Lake, and Halls Creek.

Take a trip back in time at the Double T Quik
Stop and Barbershop, where you can enjoy a small
museum with displays of old gas stations.

Four miles west of Merrillon on Highway 95 is
Alma Center, the Strawberry Capital of Wisconsin. You
will thoroughly enjoy sampling the strawberry shortcake
at the annual Strawberry Festival, held the fourth
weekend of June.

Upon leaving Alma Center stay on 95 to Hixton
and visit Cain's Orchard. Nothing tastes as good as fresh
picked fruit, and the orchard has twenty acres of apple

trees and twenty acres of Highbush blueberries. Pick your own on Saturdays during the harvest season. A gift shop displays a wide variety of merchandise.

The National Native American Vietnam Veterans Memorial at Highground is an impressive monument.

The next small town on 95 is Blair, which prides itself on its Norwegian hospitality. There is a large cheese factory and the Countryside Lefse Factory, famous for its handmade lefse using real potatoes. (Warning: Lefse is a Scandinavian flatbread, which reportedly can become addictive in a short period of time.)

From Blair CTH S takes you south to Hegg, named after a Civil War hero Col. Hans Heg. Turn West on CTH C over to Route 53 and then turn onto CTH CC and head down to the village of Ettrick.

The scenic beauty of the area reminded the early Scottish settlers of the mountainous Ettrick Forest in their homeland, and so the village got its name. Both the north and south branches of Beaver Creek flows through the town. Each August the village hosts the "Ettrick Fun Days" a celebration that lasts for three days.

A lovely winding CTH D takes you north out of Ettrick. Along the way you will pass the Fagerness Church built in 1902 and located in the exact center of Trempealeau County. Continue to follow D to the village of Whitehall.

Friday evenings are the time to visit Whitehall during the summer when you can visit the booths set up at the Farmer's Market. A variety of fresh organic produce and Amish crafts are available at the many stalls. The evening meal is provided by one of several local organizations that take turns manning the kitchen. A group of local musicians set up shop in the gazebo in the central square and you can sit at one of the many tables, enjoy your meal, and listen to some great music.

Beef and Dairy Days, held the third weekend in August features three days of fun including carnival rides, a parade, live music, and a craft show.

From Whitehall take Highway 53 up to Pigeon Falls. Both the village of Pigeon Falls and the Pigeon Creek Evangelical Lutheran Church were founded in 1866. The lovely small country church has a restored chandelier with twelve kerosene lamps, and the church is still active in the community.

Beautiful Ekern Park has several campsites and picnic areas. The park is located on the village millpond. During Memorial Day weekend it is the site of a celebration sponsored by the Pigeon Falls Lions Club.

A trip north on 53 will take you to the spectacular Buena Vista Wayside Park. From the overlook you will get a marvelous view of western Trempealeau County. If you arrive in the evening and are lucky you might be rewarded with a brilliantly-colored sunset.

Highway 53 then continues up to the town of Osseo. A must stop in Osseo is the nationally known Norske Nook Restaurant and Bakery. Established in 1973 the Norske Nook has been listed in *Roadfood* as one of the top ten cafes in the nation. It has also been named the best ethnic restaurant in the state in a reader's poll in *Wisconsin Trails* magazine. This is one destination that lives up to its reputation. When you enter the premises you can't fail to notice the enormous pie case. The biggest problem is deciding which one to try. Browsing the many antique stores and unique gift shops will help you recover from any overindulgence or work up an appetite for a return visit to the restaurant for another meal or trip to the dessert table.

You can take a rest break at Stoddard Park on the south shore of lovely Lake Martha or one of the other city parks. The third weekend in June is reserved for the "Lake Martha Days" celebration.

Turning back west Highway 10 brings you over to the town of Strum, which contains approximately 40 acres of parks and the beautiful Crystal Lake. The modern Crystal Lake Campground includes electricity, showers, and twenty-one wooded campsites.

Continuing west on Highway 10 you will come to the village of Eleva which is located on the Buffalo River in what is known as "Beef River Valley." Excellent trout fishing is available in Big Creek and Adams Creek both of which flow into Eleva pond. A trip north on Route 93 to Eleva Ridge will reward you with a fantastic view of Beef River Valley.

The first weekend in June up to 20,000 people invade the tiny village to sample some of the areas best charcoal chicken during Eleva Broiler Days.

Leaving Eleva you can travel south on 93 to CTH V. Midway on the trip down this scenic road you will pass the lovely East Bennett Valley Lutheran Church. Norwegian settlers built this church in 1909.

The Norske Nook Restaurant and Bakery is a must stop in Osseo and is one site that lives up to its reputation.

It is hard to describe a trip down CTH V, although the word corkscrew comes to mind. It is a road with continuous twists and turns and calls for an alert and skillful rider. The scenery however, is incredible.

Continuing south on V you meet up with 121 and a short jog to the west will take you to CTH Q. Turn left on Q and you are heading south again to the town of Independence.

The downtown area of Independence is dominated by the restored City Hall and Opera House. This building was completed in 1903 and is famous for its clock tower. The other well-known landmark is Saint Peter and Paul Catholic Church built in 1895.

The second weekend in June the annual Independence Days celebration is held.

Highway 93 takes you south from Independence to Arcadia. A must-stop in Arcadia is the "Avenue of Heroes Walk" in Memorial Park. Included in this fifty-four-acre park are statues and memorials to all the wars involving this country. The latest addition to the park honors those who gave their lives on 9/11 in New York City.

The East Bennet Valley Lutheran Church sits atop a small hill at the junction of CTH V and Z.

Arcadia Broiler Dairy Days is held Memorial Day weekend. Activities include a bike tour, a 4K run, carnival rides, children's events and games, and a Harley Poker Ride.

South of town on Highway 93 you will be treated to the "Wisconsin Skyline Drive" which gives breathtaking ridge top views of the pastoral valleys.

You can continue down 93 or cut off on CTH G for a winding trip south. Or a bit farther along CTH F cuts off parallel to the Highway and takes you down to Routes 35 & 54. As an alternate CTH J also takes you south out of Arcadia before it connects with G. Highway 95 west is another lovely ridge ride over to the Mississippi. There really is no way to really go wrong no matter which route you decide to take.

A statue of a mounted George Washington greets you at Memorial Park in Arcadia, Wisconsin.

Following the Mississippi north on 35 & 54 brings you to Fountain City, the site of 600-foot-high Eagle Bluff, the highest point along the Mississippi. A historic water fountain gives the city its name.

The strangest attraction in Fountain City has to be the Rock in the House, not to be confused with Spring Green's House on the Rock. In 1995 a fifty-five-ton disc-shaped rock fell from a cliff and landed in the house and there it remains. It has now been turned into a tourist site.

Elmer's Auto & Toy Museum houses over 100 classic and antique cars and a collection of over 600 children's pedal cars and tractors with many other toys on display. The museum is open two weekends a month from Memorial Day to mid-October. Check locally for the dates.

One of the largest arrowhead collections in Northwest Wisconsin is housed in the museum of the Fountain City Area Historical Society. You can also get information about the Prairie Moon Museum and Gardens.

Over 40 sculptures enclosed in a 267-foot fence are on display at Prairie Moon Museum and Gardens. The gardens are open year round but the museum is only open on Sunday afternoons from May through October.

The Fountain City Festival is held the second weekend in August, and during the same weekend there is a Polka Fest held at Hilltop Ballroom. An Old Tyme Farm Fest is held on Labor Day Weekend.

For a wonderful circle ride take Route 95 east out of Fountain City and then loop back on any of the county roads branching off from the highway. These scenic routes take you along ridges with breathtaking views, and you easily could spend a couple of days just exploring the rural roads of Buffalo County.

Just to the north of Fountain City on Highway 35 is Merrick State Park, located in the backwaters of the Mississippi, a prime fishing and waterfowl viewing area.

Continuing north to Czechville a turn to the east will give you the opportunity to enjoy the sweeping curves of Highway 88. For thirty miles you can lose yourself in the beauty of the rustic countryside until you reach a destination in the town of Mondovi.

For more lovely scenery and excellent riding you might want to head off on one of the county highways branching off from 88. CTH Z swings to the east and connects with H or a bit farther along with BB. Both of these side roads will bring you to Mondovi.

In Mondovi you can take a break at one of the five lovely parks, go back in time at the School Museum and Rural Life Museum, or try your hand at fishing in Mirror Lake.

Friendship Days provides a great time over the Fourth of July; the Buffalo County Fair is held during the first week in August.

Once again there are so many county highways in the Mondovi area that you will find it hard to be disappointed no matter which ones you choose to explore. Highway 37 south is also great ride along the Buffalo River.

For a peaceful site you might want to check out the old mill and waterfall in Modena, a small town on Highway 37 south of Mondovi.

Continue south on 37 to CTH N and then follow that back to the Mississippi River just above Buffalo City. A short jog south on 35 and a turn onto CTH O will take you to the town, which is located close along the river.

Closely adjacent towns Cochran and Buffalo City share a great Fourth of July celebration, and on Labor Day weekend the Buffalo City Bash is held. There are several parks where you can stop to relax including Foelsch Riverside Park where you can hike the nature trails and enjoy the views of the bluffs.

Follow CTH OO north for a scenic ride along the backwaters of the river until it joins up with 35 for a ride up to Alma.

The town of Alma is a popular spot to stop for a rest or an overnight stay. One distinctive feature of the town is the buildings carved into the bluff. Another point of interest is the 10 steep staircases that link Main Street with Second Street.

At Buena Vista Park a natural viewing platform atop the 500-foot promontory gives a wonderful view of the town, the Mississippi River, and the surrounding valleys and palisades.

Camping is available at Rieck's Lake to the north of town. There are also a wildlife observation platform and interpretive panels. If you wish to cool off you can visit the public swimming beach at Alma Marina or stand on the viewing platform and watch the boats and barges passing through at Lock and Dam #4.

The Alma Area Museum holds a wealth of local history including a detailed logging exhibit and an original Alma baseball team uniform plus the silver trophy won by the team in 1927. You may pick up a brochure for a self-guided tour that will take you to several homes listed on the National Register of Historic Places. Most of these homes are now Bed and Breakfast establishments.

Back on Highway 35 you continue upriver to the village of Nelson where you will want to stop at the Nelson Cheese Factory. For five generations the company has produced delicious, Colby, Cheddar, and Monterey Jack cheeses, and fresh curd. For those interested in learning more about the cheese making process, there is an observation window into the factory. Also in Nelson is the Tiffany Wildlife Area. For those seeking a bit more adventure, you can try hang gliding.

Crossing the Chippewa River you follow 35 to the town of Pepin, located on the shores of Lake Pepin. For those who grew up watching "Little House on Prairie" this will be of particular interest since this is the home of the Laura Ingalls Wilder Museum. During the third full weekend in September, the town celebrates Laura Ingalls Wilder Days which honors the life of the famous children's author. The Little House Wayside, marks Laura's birthplace, and was the location of her book "The Little House in the Big Woods." The wayside is found seven miles from Pepin on CTH CC. Charles and Caroline Ingalls once owned this parcel of land, and a replica of the log cabin where Laura was born has been built at this site.

In May you can enjoy bird watching during the Great River Birding Festival, and throughout the summer and fall live theater is presented by the Lake Pepin Players.

The authentic 111-year-old railroad depot is home to the Pepin Depot Museum where the history of railroading and steamships can be found in the many displays.

From Pepin take CTH N and head north until you reach CTH D. Here be prepared for a dazzling ride with the road swiftly taking you from the floor of Plum Creek Valley to Columbia Heights ridge and down to Porcupine Valley and then up once more over another ridge to Big Coulee before leading back out into the prairie to rejoin N.

This tiny cabin is a replica of the birthplace of Laura Ingalls Wilder.

By the time that N takes you to the hamlet of Arkansas you will be ready for a quiet rest at Arkansas Creek Park. The park follows a stream through a steep, narrow gorge, which was once the site of logging and grain milling operations.

If you take CTH Z to X and turn north to Eau Galle, a wonderful scenic ride leads you to a dam across the Eau Galle River, and this is worth the few minutes spent to take this route. The town of Eau Galle itself is a lovely village beside the small lake. For the romantic the Lakeside Wedding Chapel would be the spot for a memorable ceremony. There is also a pleasant city park alongside the dam.

From Eau Galle take D to Route 25 but be sure to swing into the wayside just north of the junction for a panoramic view of the Chippewa River bottoms and Waubeek Mound.

The Depot Museum in Pepin, Wisconsin, has informative displays telling the history of railroading and steamships along the river.

About ten miles up 25 is Downsville, home to The Creamery Restaurant & Inn, which features homemade meals prepared with fresh seasonal ingredients. This restaurant has twice been named to the Milwaukee Journal's list of Wisconsin's twenty-five best restaurants, and you can enjoy your meal in the dining room, the lounge or the outdoor garden terrace.

Turn west onto 72 and travel over to Elmwood for an out-of-this-world experience. Several UFO sightings in the late 1970's gave Elmwood the title of "UFO Capital of the World." During the last weekend in July, the residents celebrate "UFO Days," and although this northern Roswell doesn't promise you will meet any aliens, the human residents will serve you their famous "UFO Burgers."

For a more distant history, a one hundred-year-old log house stands on Public Street across from the Catholic Church.

The Lakeside Wedding Chapel draws couples looking for a lovely setting for their special day.

Continue west on 72 about five miles to CTH S which takes you down to Plum City, which got its name from a profusion of wild plum trees that grew in the valley.

You can pick up CTH U in Plum City and head over to CC and on to J which will take you to

Stockholm where you can examine the works of the town's many resident artists and crafters or you can stay on S as it winds its way down to Maiden Rock and meets up with Route 35 at the Mississippi.

If you opt to visit Stockholm, the famous Stockholm Art Festival is held the third Saturday in July. Over one hundred artists display their work in the city park, and you can find original fine art at reasonable prices.

You can then follow 35 to Maiden Rock, named after Winona, the Indian maiden who threw herself from a nearby bluff rather than marry a man she didn't love. The third Saturday in June is Summerfest time in Maiden Rock. This gala celebration offers fun for visitors of all ages.

A colorful fireworks display, reflected in the waters of Lake Pepin, is a sight you won't want to miss on the Fourth of July.

The welcome mat is rolled out for motorcyclists in April and September when Maiden Rock is a favorite stop for bikers riding the Flood Run, a charitable event which raises money for Gillette Children's Hospital and attracts up to 7500 riders.

Three miles up 35 from Maiden Rock is a wayside that is worth a stop. As you look south two bluffs jutting out into the river give the impression of a gateway through which the river meanders on its way.

It is easy to pass by Bay City, located just off of 35, but take time to cross the railroad tracks to enjoy the beautiful riverside park. Visit some of the historic buildings still standing which include the Conlin log cabin built in 1856 by an Irish immigrant, the River Bluffs Historical Center located next door in a renovated church or you may want to visit the old jail or the original grain elevator. Several of the early homes also grace the village.

The village holds the Bay City Days during the first weekend in June, a fun-filled celebration for all ages.

Continuing north towards Hager City you will come to an interesting historical marker just south of town. A huge bow and arrow fashioned out of rocks is visible on the bluff. There is much speculation as to the meaning of the icon as it seems the arrow is pointed at Lake Pepin. The speculation of the rider is as plausible as any since no one really knows the meaning of the formation.

The hamlet of Diamond Bluff lies a few miles farther north. The disastrous voyage of the Sea Wing began in Diamond Bluff and a historical marker tells of the tragedy. On the waterfront the Gem, the town's only bar and grill, supplies excellent food and a wonderful view of the river.

Remain on 35 heading north to CTH E for a trip up to River Falls.

During July and August, football fans will want to check out the summer training camp of the Kansas City Chiefs where spectators may watch the daily practice sessions at no charge.

Other points of interest in River Falls include Kinnickinnic River, one of the premier trout streams of the Upper Midwest; Hoffman and Mound Parks; and excellent shopping and dining on the main street. The Old Falls theatre offers new films at old time prices.

Three miles south of River Falls you can connect with Highway 29 for a side loop over to Spring Valley.

Traveling bikers round a scenic curve overlooking the river at Diamond Bluff.

The town of Spring Valley is the site of the 640-acre Eau Galle Recreation Area which offers a multitude of outdoor activities including camping, swimming, hiking, picnicking, fishing, or the opportunity just to sit quietly beside Lake George and enjoy nature.

Eau Galle Recreation Area was created when the Army Corps of Engineers built a flood control dam, the largest earthen dam in the Midwest across Mines Creek. Approximately a quarter of a million yearly visitors are attracted to the park's scenic lake, rugged bluffs, and picturesque valley.

In mid-September the village celebrates Spring Valley Dam Days, which includes free entertainment, two mile and 10 K runs, parade, beer garden, antique car show, and plenty of good food.

Crystal Cave, Wisconsin's longest cave, is located one mile west of Spring Valley on 29 for those who enjoy exploring underground. Here you can take an hour-long guided tour, pan for gemstones or indulge your sweet tooth at the gift and fudge store.

A short trip west on 29 will bring you to CTH CC and turn to the south to CTH C. A right turn takes you west to CTH N and over to Highway 65. Take 65 south to the town of Ellsworth, the county seat for Pierce County.

In 1984 former governor Anthony S. Earl named Ellsworth, where the annual Cheese Curd Festival is held in June, as the Cheese Curd Capitol of Wisconsin The town also hosts the popular Polka Fest early in July and the Pierce County Fairgrounds is the site of the Beldenville Old Car Club Show at the end of the month.

Take Highway 10 west from Ellsworth over to Prescott, located at the mouth of the St. Croix River. Here you might enjoy a visit to Kinnickinnic State Park before crossing the St. Croix into Minnesota.

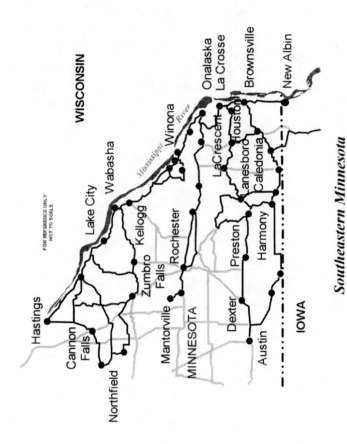

CHAPTER SEVEN

MARVELOUS MINNESOTA

There is much to see in the southeastern corner of Minnesota. As you cross into the state you'll encounter the pristine waters at the mouth of a wild river. You can visit the town of Northfield, the Waterloo of the James/Younger gang of outlaws, and you can get acquainted with live bald eagles at Wabasha. If you love exquisite woodcarving, you'll be awed by the intricate work on a hand-carved carousel, or you can relax and enjoy the forest of masts in the largest inland marina on the Mississippi. You can ride either a scenic four-lane highway or explore countless winding back roads.

The sapphire of the St. Croix River, as it flows into the Mississippi, is a sharp contrast to the dun color of the big river. As soon as you cross into Minnesota, you can stop at the small park, take a break, and look upstream from the mouth of the St. Croix. The St. Croix has been designated a wild river and commercial exploitation is prohibited. For the most part the St. Croix is best explored by boat.

Continue west on Route 10 to 61 South, where you will cross the Mississippi at the town of Hastings.

Hastings marks the conjunction of three rivers: the St. Croix, the Mississippi, and the Vermillion. In town, sixty-two buildings are included in the National Historic Registry. The restored Dakota County Courthouse now houses the Hastings City Hall; in the downtown area many of the historic buildings are now occupied by a variety of shops.

The small park just inside the Minnesota state line is a great place to rest and watch pleasure boats on the beautiful St. Croix River.

The town and surrounding area offer several parks, among them Spring Lake Park northwest of the city, which features hiking trails along with the Schaar's Bluff Picnic Area where you can eat lunch while enjoying a wonderful view of the Mississippi. More hiking trails are in Afton State Park, or a close-up view of the Mississippi can be found at spring-fed Lake Rebecca.

Don't miss Vermillion Falls. You won't forget standing on the observation platform and looking down the narrow limestone ravine to where the water roars over the falls.

In mid July, Rivertown Days features a lumberjack show, carnival, flea market, parades, and other festivities.

Take county Highway 18 South through the river bottoms. You might want to stop and try your luck at the Treasure Island gambling boat or you can continue on to Highway 61.

A short jaunt on Highway 61 takes you to 19 West, a road with a few sweeping curves and an easy, scenic ride over to Cannon Falls. Or you can turn west for a few miles and connect with CR 7 which also will give you a nice scenic ride south to meet up with 19 and then over to Cannon Falls.

Minnieska Park is located on the banks of the Little Cannon River and is worth a relaxing stop. The park provides a great view of the stair-step falls. While there stop at the nearby Stone Mill Coffeehouse and Eatery and browse a European style coffeehouse, a marketplace for unique gifts and art objects, a dinner theater, and a restaurant overlooking the falls.

During the second weekend in July, the Cannon Falls Arts Festival brings in local and visiting artists displaying their wares. The first Sunday in August is reserved for the Cannon Cruising Days Car Show.

One of Minnesota's first Swedish American settlements, Cannon Falls celebrates its history at the Vasa Museum. The 1901 building has been restored and has long been a prominent source of Swedish-American Culture.

Those interested in the "wild west" will want to continue on 19 to the town of Northfield which secured its place in the history books September 7, 1876, when eight members of the infamous James-Younger gang rode into town to rob the bank. Heroic bank teller Joseph Heywood refused to open the safe and was killed while local citizens fought to protect their town and thwarted the robbery. Two members of the gang were killed on the street and the others fled. Although Jesse and Frank James were able to escape back to Missouri, the three Younger brothers were captured and sentenced to long prison terms.

A path beside the Little Cannon River gives a wonderful view of the rushing water as it tumbles over the stair-step falls.

"The Defeat of Jesse James Days" is held annually the first weekend after Labor Day. The attempted bank robbery is re-enacted during the celebration and is dedicated to the memory of Joseph Heywood. The Northfield Historical Society is located next to the restored First National Bank which still bears bullet holes from that fateful raid.

The attempted bank robbery site is not the only point of interest in Northfield; the town is also home to two excellent colleges. Northfield residents always have believed strongly in education and in 1866 founded Northfield College, now called Carleton College. In 1874 Norwegian settlers founded St. Olaf College, still recognized as a seat of Norwegian culture.

You may wish to take the self-guided tour of the many historic homes and buildings, explore the interesting shops, or take a few minutes to enjoy nature. You can end the day with a meal at one of the many restaurants and spend the evening attending a concert or enjoying some live theater.

A sign in the Northfield Historical Society Museum tells the story of the defeat of the James-Younger Gang in 1876.

Upon leaving Northfield, Highway 246S will take you down to Nerstrand Big Woods State Park. The only working dairy farm in a state park is just one of the features at Nerstrand. This eighty-acre farm is leased to a family who helps educate the public about the results of sustainable farming practices.

In the Spring this park is a huge wildflower garden, so be sure to stroll the boardwalk through this floral wonderland. Among the many varieties of flowers, you may see delicate flowers like the endangered dwarf trout lily, endemic to this region. There is a $50,000 fine for knowingly harming one of these plants.

From Nerstrand stay on 246 to CR 30 and take that over to CR 1. Follow this road over to Red Wing.

Red Wing is a town with a little something for everyone. If you are interested in natural history, archeology, shopping, recreation, arts and culture, history, good eating, or just enjoying the river and the surrounding bluffs, you will find it in Red Wing. For detailed information regarding Red Wing, stop at the old railroad depot. The friendly and knowledgeable staff can let you know about the many current activities and events planned. The depot is also still in use as the Amtrak station and is the home of the Red Wing Arts Association Gallery.

Red Wing is also well known as the home of Red Wing Shoes, as well as for its fine pottery and stoneware. In several places you are welcome to watch as the pottery and stoneware are made. It is easy to spend a day shopping in the malls and the unique shops and galleries located throughout the town.

One of the finest permanent art collections in the Midwest is found at the Anderson Center for Interdisciplinary Studies. Signed and numbered original prints by Picasso, Dali, Chagall, Warhol, and many other artists are on display.

The Red Wing Depot serves many purposes: visitor's center, Amtrak station, and art gallery.

Red Wing also is home to the Sheldon Performing Arts Theater; the beautifully-restored 1904 theater attracts fine nationally-known acts and displays the talents of a very active community theater group.

For a view of the city and the Mississippi, be sure to head up to Sorin Bluff to the scenic overlook. For those with an interest in paleontology or archeology, the area is rich with fossils and artifacts of the early Native Americans. A visit to the Goodhue County Museum will help to acquaint you with the first inhabitants of Red Wing. Red Wing also features nearly fifty restaurants, so whatever your preference in dining might be, you'll likely find it here. Lodging runs the gamut from B&Bs in Victorian manors to modern motel chains.

In April and September Red Wing welcomes thousands of bikers during the Flood Runs. In the latter part of May the city holds the Great Minnesota Morel Festival;

avid morel hunters and eaters definitely will not want to miss this event.

Route 61 follows the river south, skirting the shores of Lake Pepin. A nice rest stop can be found at Frontenac State Park where you can do a bit of hiking or enjoy some bird watching.

A few miles farther down 61 brings you to Lake City and the largest small craft marina on the Mississippi. A pleasant stroll along the two and a half mile waterfront will give you ample opportunity to inspect the moored boats. At twenty-one miles long and three miles across, Lake Pepin is the widest stretch of the Mississippi River.

In 1922 history was made and a new sport born when an eighteen-year-old resident, Ralph Samuelson, attached a pair of pine boards to his feet and was pulled across the lake behind a speedboat. This event is commemorated each year during the last weekend in June when Lake City celebrates Water Ski Days. Many of the shops and eateries in Lake City feature a nautical theme.

Wildlife abounds in the bluffs around Lake City, and Hok-Si-La Park along the river edge is a great place for bird watching or camping.

Although water sports are the main focus of Lake City, the town also is the starting point for several excellent motorcycle roads.

The main road south is, of course, Highway 61. On this picturesque road you will follow the Mississippi closely, although on weekends it can be very busy. As alternatives, several county roads leading through the Richard J. Dorer Memorial Hardwood State Forest will give you nice sweeping rides with much less traffic.

Just north of Lake City you can turn west onto CR 5 and enjoy a scenic ride over to Highway 58. A left turn onto 58 will take you down to the town of Zumbroto.

A forest of masts is visible at the largest small craft marina on the Mississippi at Lake City, MN.

Many historic buildings remain in Zumbroto, including a Carnegie Library built in 1906 and the State Theater. The only remaining covered bridge in Minnesota can be found at the sixty-eight-acre Covered Bridge Park. This 116-foot-long bridge was built in 1869 and was moved to its present location in 1997. Other historic buildings in the park include the Milwaukee RR Depot and a one-room schoolhouse.

In Zumbroto you can join up with Highway 60 east for a wonderful thirty-seven-mile ride over to Wabasha. Wide sweeping curves and some tighter turns will keep you alert.

You also can leave Lake City on CR 9 and wind your way south to CR 11 which takes you over to 63 North and up to connect with 60.

An alternate route out of Lake City is to head south a couple of miles and then turn onto CR 4 which twists along the bluffs for a short ride before heading off to the west. Turning onto SR 10 you will find an exhilarating ride through sweeping curves back over to 61 at Read's Landing, just north of Wabasha.

At Read's Landing there is a pullout and river overlook platform where you can stop for a rest and perhaps spot a bald eagle.

Movie buffs will want to visit "Slippery's" Bar & Grill in Wabasha, the site used for the "Grumpy Old Men" movies. But there are many more points of interest in the town, where only about a fourth of the buildings were built after 1900. The entire downtown area is designated as a National Historic District.

The National Eagle Center downtown will allow you to get a close-up view of Harriet, Angel, and Columbia, three bald eagles whose permanently damaged wings make it impossible to release them back into the wild. One of the highest concentrations of bald eagles in the lower forty-eight states can be found in the Wabasha area.

Slippery's Bar & Grill was the site of the movie "Grumpy Old Men." The two main characters were based on two local, colorful residents of Wabasha.

A few miles south of Wabasha on Highway 61 is the village of Kellogg and where a must-stop is Lark Toy Company, the world's largest specialty store. Turn on CR 18 and then make an immediate left onto Lark Lane. You'll be taken back to childhood when you see the magnificent hand-carved carousel featuring nineteen whimsical animals. (The difference between a carousel and merry-go-round? A merry-go-round has only horses, while a carousel features a menagerie of creatures.) The carousel runs once every hour.

Bald eagle Angel demonstrates her impressive wingspan at the National Eagle Center in Wabasha, MN.

Watch excited children enjoy riding the colorful carousel while you have lunch in the excellent small restaurant. Choose from cotton candy, burgers, fries, and a maddening assortment of delectable cookies.

Several more wonderfully hand-carved and exquisitely painted creatures are on display throughout the store and museum.

A series of connected rooms, each with its own theme, will delight children of all ages. The entire complex covers over thirty thousand square feet. One fascinating room houses the Moose Tracks Museum, which displays twenty-five thousand antique toys dating from the early 1900s to the 1960s. For outdoor fun there is a challenging miniature golf course.

During the weekend after Labor Day, Kellogg celebrates the annual four-day Watermelon Fest when activities include carnival rides, a flea market, the kiddies' parade on Saturday, and a grand parade on Sunday.

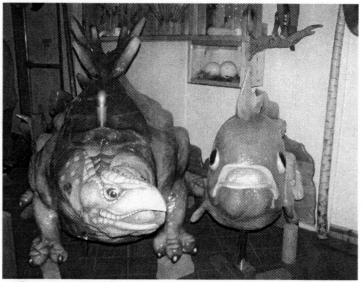

A dinosaur and a fish are just two of the hand-carved, magical creatures that inhabit the Lark Toy Company.

To the south of town are 700 acres of prairie sand dunes managed by the Nature Conservancy. Conscientious visitors are welcome to stop by and view the wildflowers and native prairie grasses, and to try to spot the rare Blanding's Turtle.

High bluffs to the west and the Mississippi to the east flank the four lanes of Highway 61 heading down to

Winona, Minnesota's largest river city. Although an excellent road and very scenic this route is extremely busy, and exercising caution is prudent.

For a fun circle ride turn off Rt. 61 and onto 248 over to Rollingstone, a hamlet which celebrates its ethnic roots at the Rollingstone Luxembourg Heritage Museum, housed in the former jail.

From Rollingstone take CR 25 and head through a nice series of sweeping turns down to a left turn onto CR 20 and another series of curves over to Stockton. George Hinton Memorial Park in Stockton is a nice place to take a break in the shade of a large pavilion. CR 23 takes you north and back to Rt. 61 or you can head over to Winona on Rt. 14, which is a nice curvy highway that also joins up with Rt. 61.

If you approach Winona from the north, a right turn off of 61 onto Garvin Heights Road will take you up a bluff towering five hundred seventy-five feet above the city. From here Winona gives the appearance of an island community, bordered on the east by the Mississippi and on the west by Lake Winona. The panoramic view from Garvin Heights allows you see twenty to thirty miles up and down the river.

While coming down from Garvin Heights, the road changes to Huff Road as you cross 61. The Winona Visitor Center at the intersection of 61 and Huff will be an informative stop.

The visitor center, a band shell, Veteran's Park, and a formal rose garden all are located in Lake Park which surrounds the lake. You also get a great view of the Sugarloaf, an unusual eighty-five-foot high rock formation atop a 500-foot bluff. This landmark for riverboat pilots was created by quarrymen in the 1800s.

Over one hundred National Historic Registry sites grace the downtown area, many of which are decorated with beautiful stained glass windows. Tiffany Studios in

New York designed the stained glass and bronze work adorning the Winona National Bank.

Other structures with ornate stained glass windows include The Merchants Bank, a 1915 Prairie School-style building, and the Watkins Company administration building. The Watkins Heritage Museum tells the story of the company and displays memorabilia along with current products. A block away from the Watkins building is the Polish Cultural Institute which celebrates the Polish immigrants' impact on the history of Winona.

A walk through the downtown area provides ample opportunity for shopping, eating, and viewing historic buildings. You can take a break in the gazebo in at Windom Park; admire the statue of Princess We-no-nah, which is part of the restored fountain; and enjoy the colorful flowerbeds. The park is bordered on three sides by large Victorian homes.

In Levee Park on the Mississippi waterfront you can explore the C. Wilkie Steamboat Museum. This is a must-stop for anyone with an interest in the history of river travel.

Several festivals and celebrations are also part of the fun of Winona. In May Polish Heritage Days are observed, and in June the town honors the river heritage with Steamboat Days. Two celebrations are held in September: the "World's Fair" recognizes the cultural diversity of the area, and the Winona Historical Society sponsors a Victorian Fair. In October, "Smaczne Jablka" (tasty apple)—otherwise known as Polish Apple Day—is held, along with the Big Muddy River Rendezvous. In August, the neighboring town of Goodview holds Goodview Days.

Stay on 61 South to CR 7 and visit historic Pickwick Mill, on Lake LaBelle, two miles from 61. Construction of the mill was started in 1854 and completed in 1858. The name "Pickwick Mill" was chosen in 1857 by Mary Davis after she had read Charles Dickens' *Pickwick Papers*. The mill is open weekends during May, September, and October and daily in June, July, and August. Visitors will enjoy the six floors of original machinery, the four-foot-by-twenty-foot water wheel, and the operating millstones. A nearby restaurant offers good food and a view of the falls.

A replica of the steamboat Julius C. Wilkie houses the Steamboat Museum in Winona, MN.

Pickwick holds "Mill Day" on the second Saturday in September.

Continue on CR 7, then drop down to CR 12 to get to Great River Bluffs State Park. The ride to the park follows a ridge bordered by deep valleys that are very scenic, but be prepared: before reaching the park, the road turns to gravel and remains gravel throughout the park.

An alternate route from Winona is to take Highway 14 west to Rochester, the largest city in Southern Minnesota. In Rochester you may take a behind-the-scenes tour of the world famous Mayo Clinic or a tour of Mayowood, the mansion called home by three generations of the Mayo family. Another historic home, open to the public on Wednesday afternoons from June through August, is the Tudor style home of Dr. Henry S. Plummer. A tour includes the forty-nine-room mansion and eleven acres of landscaped grounds.

The Pickwick Mill is the one of the oldest gristmills in Southeastern MN. During the Civil War, it operated twenty-four hours a day providing flour for the Union troops.

In contrast, Heritage House, located in Rochester's Town Square Central Park, gives visitors a glimpse into the life of a middle-class family of one hundred years ago.

Cultural attractions in Rochester include a symphony orchestra, art center, theaters, and the Mayo Civic Center, which offers performances by A-list entertainers.

The view from the approach road to Great River Bluffs State Park is spectacular.

A short trip farther west on 14 will take you to 57 and a ride up to Mantorville. A must stop is Hubbell House, a restaurant which has been luring travelers and locals with excellent food since 1864. In addition to experiencing the fantastic food at the Hubbell House, be sure to browse the antique and specialty shops, check out the Chocolate Shoppe with its hand-dipped chocolate, and inspect the 1800s architecture.

You can then work off the effects of dinner and chocolate by taking a stroll around the lovely city park, inspecting the covered bridge, watching the Canada Geese, and enjoying the water rushing over the dam.

Drop back down to Route 14 and circle back to Rochester to catch 52 down to I-90 and a fast trip back to the Mississippi.

Whether you take I-90 from Rochester or come down from Great River Bluffs State Park, you will want to take CR 12 through Nodine. This route starts out a bit rough, but it smoothes out, and at the end the two-mile stretch of twists down to Dakota will have you scraping the pegs. Once you reach the bottom take a moment to catch your breath, then turn around and go back up and enjoy a whole different perspective. At the top take CR 1 (also known as the Apple Blossom Drive) along the top of the bluffs. This winds through orchards and gives tantalizing glimpses of the river before dropping down to LaCrescent.

Known as the Apple Capital of Minnesota, the first orchards were planted in the LaCrescent area in the 1850s, and in early May the apple blossoms are in full bloom. You can also enjoy a view of the river and Lake Onalaska from an overlook at the top of the bluff. From late summer throughout the fall fresh crisp apples are available at many roadside stands.

From LaCrescent take SR 16 south and west. This road is also known as the Historic Bluff Country Scenic Byway and winds for eighty-eight miles to the town of Dexter.

At the village of Hokah, Como Falls is located near Mount Tom in a quiet little park at the edge of town. Further along the way you'll want to stop at the Houston Nature Center and visit Alice, a Great Horned Owl. Alice suffered permanent damage to her wing when she was only three weeks old, but she now helps at the center with educational programs. The first weekend in March the center holds the Festival of Owls with educational programs given by owl researchers and other experts. Included in this event is a hatch day party for Alice.

The eighteen-acre center is planted with native prairie and wetland plant species and also displays an unusual collection of REBART (Recycled Bicycle Art).

While in Houston, stop in at Cody's Mercantile and sample some bison and wild boar. The business is named after Cody the Buffalo, which had a starring role

in the movies *Dances With Wolves* and *Radio Flyer*. He
has also appeared in several commercials. It is reported
that Cody's charging scenes are filmed by placing his
favorite food, Oreo cookies, off camera and allowing
Cody to run towards the treats.

*This model John Deere Tractor is one of the whimsical creations of
REBART on the grounds of the Houston Minnesota Nature Center.*

Another side trip will take you from Houston
south on SR 76 to CR 4, a road with nice sweeping
curves along the valley floor to Spring Grove.
Attractions in Spring Grove include the Ballard House
Museum and a park housing a Christmas Village during
the holiday season.

Head east on Rt. 44 from Spring Grove to
Caledonia and visit Beaver Creek Valley State Park
which will give you an opportunity to get off the bikes
and enjoy a pleasant hike among the bluffs. The park also
has an excellent campground.

This Viking Warrior stands guard at the "Wood Spinner Shop and Gallery" in Spring Grove.

Caledonia north on Highway 76 is a fun ride of twelve miles through the valley and back to Houston to rejoin Route 16 west.

Sweeping curves continue as you head over to Rushford. As you approach, you will notice the name of the town prominently displayed on a nearby bluff. For more information on the area you can stop at the visitor's center in the restored 1867 railway depot.

Four miles west is the town of Peterson. Both towns offer many outdoor activities and take advantage of their location close to the scenic Root River. There are several campgrounds ranging from primitive to modern; for more luxury you might want to stay at Lillian's House of the Seven Gables, Peterson's oldest house, which is now a B&B.

Route 16 continues twisting along the banks of the Root River from Peterson to Lanesboro, the "Little Town in the Valley." Lanesboro has dining and lodging for every taste and budget. Most of the downtown area is listed on the National Registry of Historic Places. You can find much local heritage at the Lanesboro Historical Museum and you can enjoy live performances at the famous Commonweal Theater. The area also is home to a sizeable Amish population and their handmade wares are available in several of local shops.

The beautiful Sylvan Park with its spring-fed trout ponds, campground, rest rooms, electricity, picnic shelters, and a flock of friendly ducks make it one of the best city parks in Minnesota. Several annual festivals, including the Sykkle Tour in May, Art in the Park on Father's Day, August's Buffalo Bill Days, and Oktoberfest provide a fun time for visitors and townspeople alike.

It is easy to spend a day investigating all the shops in the town. Or you might like to take a tour of the Lanesboro Fish Hatchery, which is located south of town. This is one of five state-run coldwater fish hatcheries in Minnesota and raises trout for release in the area's lakes and rivers. For a different view of the village take a trolley tour through the town and the agricultural countryside.

Taking 16 West out of Lanesboro you make a climb up to Inspiration Point, a large rest area with wonderful views of the surrounding valleys. No matter which way you look, you will get a panoramic view of the countryside.

For another fun ride take a side trip from Lanesboro up Route 250. After crossing the bridge over the Root River you will find nine miles of road that include a bit of everything. Twists, sweeps and hills will hold your attention along 250 as you head north to Route 30. The ride back to Lanesboro is just as much fun.

The bridge over the Root River in Lanesboro leads you to a twisting ride up Route 250.

Another challenging ride is CR 21 heading south from Lanesboro to Canton. Just outside of Lanesboro are some wonderful sweeps and further along are a series of hills as you near Canton. You will want to stay alert on these roads, as you will be sharing the routes with the Amish and their horses and buggies.

Take Route 44 over to Harmony, "The Biggest Little Town in Southern Minnesota." Here you will find the largest Amish community in Minnesota.

Over 4000 items including many small antique toys are housed in the Harmony Toy Museum.

One more site you won't want to miss is Niagara Cave, one of the top ten rated caves in the country. A one-hour guided tour will take you to the sixty-foot waterfall, the Crystal Wedding Chapel, the stalactite room, and a chance to study various fossils. The ten-acre grounds include a picnic area and a chance to mine for real gemstones and fossils. To get to the cave, take 139 S and turn west on CR 30.

After the visit to the cave return to Harmony and

take Highway 52 up to Preston.

The town of Preston features one of the Midwest's most unusual B&Bs. The Jailhouse Inn is located in the restored 1869 Filmore County Jail. You can choose to sleep in the cellblock, the courtroom, or the Sheriff's personal bedroom.

You can head west on 16 to CR 5 or take the more winding CR 14 over to 5 but either way will take you to Forestville and Mystery Cave State Park. Be prepared to hit gravel on the road to the state park. A naturalist will take you on a tour of the cave. With the temperature at a constant 48 degrees, it would be wise to wear a jacket while exploring below ground.

You can then cross the Carnegie Steel Bridge and enter a piece of living history with the re-created village of Forestville. Costumed guides will take you through the village, populated by people portraying the original settlers. The village contains many restored buildings and a heritage garden where no modern hybrid seeds are used, so the vegetables are those that would have been grown over a hundred years ago.

Returning to Highway 16 you continue west to the village of Spring Valley which was the home of the Wilder family, and The Methodist Church where the family worshiped now houses the Wilder Museum. Laura and Almanzo Wilder and their daughter Rose lived for about a year in Spring Valley in 1890. The museum displays the village heritage along with the Wilder's history.

The scenic ride along Highway 16 ends at the town of Dexter, where you can join up with I-90. However, you might want to make a visit to a rather interesting truck stop and rest area. The station and a restaurant are built around an attractive Dutch windmill theme.

A short trip on I-90 west will take you to Austin,

a city with a lot to offer. The town is the home to the Hormel Company and its free Spam Museum, a major stop, where you will find all things Spam. The exterior of the Museum features an Old Market design; inside you will find a retail store with a selection of Spam merchandise, a video presentation, a conveyer belt filled with cans of Spam and an interesting history of Spam. The film clip of the funniest Spam moment, a Monty Python skit involving Spam, also is shown.

A friendly can of Spam welcomes visitors to the Spam Museum in Austin.

You can also visit the Hormel Historic Home, originally constructed in 1871. The Austin Area Commission is renovating the Paramount Theater for the Arts, an art and film center.

The Mower County Fair Grounds houses over twenty different historical facilities which include exhibits on Native American artifacts, a fireman tribute, a pioneer museum, a collection of horse-drawn carriages, and many other historical displays.

The history of bicycles can be found at the Rydjor Bike Museum. You can find over fifty bikes, including the 1868 "Boneshaker" at the museum.

Austin is home to 28 parks. The Jay C. Hormel Nature Center is a 278-acre facility with an interpretive center and a three-story observation tower. In August, the annual Ethnic Fest is held at the city Welcome Center at Todd Park.

Take I-90 back east to Highway 56 and then head south and east just north of the Iowa state line. At the village of LeRoy, you might want to stop at Lake Louise State Park, Minnesota's oldest continuous recreation area. LeRoy also boasts a Prairie School Bank designed by the noted architects Purcell and Elmse and a 1915 Carnegie Public Library.

Continue east on Route 56 to Route 63 and go three miles north to CR 14 and a return trip to Harmony. From there Route 44 takes you back to Caledonia.

At Caledonia take CR 3 over to Brownsville. There are some really nice sweeps at both ends of this smooth, blacktopped road. From Brownsville you can follow along between the bluffs and the Mississippi as you head south on Route 26 into Iowa. Or you can chose to take CR 16 on a panoramic ride along the tops of a ridge from Spring Grove to the state line, where it turns into county road A16 before suddenly dropping down to Dorchester, Iowa.

Northeastern Iowa

CHAPTER EIGHT

IOWA: MORE THAN JUST CORNFIELDS

If the word "Iowa" brings up an image of nothing but flat land and cornfields, this northeast corner of the state will alter your thinking. Here the bluffs are some of the highest along the river. From the incredible overlook at Mt. Hosmer in Lansing to your double-take when you happen upon the life size pink elephant between McGregor and Marquette, this section of the river will be full of surprises.

Riding down the bluff to Dorchester on A16 gives a bird's eye view of the charming small town nestled in the hollow. At the south edge of the hamlet you connect with Highway 76 and head south for a few miles to County Road A26, a great road with challenging twists and turns along the valley floor. There is a about a half mile patch of gravel, but if you can handle that short stretch, the rewards of the road are well worth the effort.

You then reach Highway 26, just south of New Albin, a small town right on the Minnesota border. A few miles down 26 you will find Fish Farm Mounds State Preserve which shows the work of the prehistoric Native American mound builders.

Six miles south of Fish Farm Mounds is the village of Lansing, a small town containing a couple of fascinating sites. For anyone with an interest in the development of a typical Mississippi River town, a must-stop is the Commercial Fishing Museum where exhibits include steam-boating, the pearl button industry, commercial fishing, and the winter ice harvests.

Brave riders may make the trek to Mt. Hosmer City Park. Hairpin turns climbing up the bluff will have you scraping the pegs, but the views of the river and town from the top are spectacular. There is also a World War I memorial on the park grounds.

The WW I Memorial sits atop the bluff at Mt. Hosmer Park in Lansing, Iowa.

From Lansing take CR X52 south for a scenic ride through the bluff country to Harper's Ferry or take Highway 9 west to Waukon, stopping for a quick snack at the cheese store in Churchtown.

You can discover Waukon's past at the Allamakee County Historical Center in the restored courthouse which also houses the Old Courthouse Museum. Among the exhibits are a

The bluffs almost disappear in the fog from the overlook on the road twisting up to Mt. Hosmer.

a Victorian parlor, Native American artifacts, an old courtroom, and an antique kitchen. A fully restored log cabin also is located on the site.

A half-mile south of Waukon you will find Sweeney's House of Clocks. It is open by appointment only but inside are almost 1000 antique and handmade clocks.

For those needing parts or an oil change, Waukon Power Sports on Route 9 has a full service center.

You can turn either east or west on CR A52 out of Waukon, but by turning west you can explore a nice loop that takes you over to Decorah.

Decorah is a town which celebrates its Norwegian heritage. The Vesterheim Norwegian American Museum is the most comprehensive ethnic museum in the U.S. where over 21,000 artifacts relating to the Norwegian experience in Northern Iowa can be found. You also can take classes in Norwegian culture and folk art.

The annual Nordic Fest, a rollicking, three-day festival featuring Norwegian art, dancing, and food, is held at the end of July. Luther College, an undergraduate liberal arts school, also is located in Decorah.

The Porter House Museum, a large Victorian home and grounds surrounded by an unusual rock wall, houses a large collection of butterflies, moths, insects, and rocks. For those who like to stroll through beautiful gardens, a visit to the Willowglen Nursery is in order. The large display gardens show off new and unusual plants along with ornamental and basket willows.

A trip up Highway 52 takes you to Burr Oak and the Laura Ingalls Wilder Park and Museum. The Ingalls family moved to Burr Oak in 1876, when Laura was nine years old and where Charles Ingalls managed the Burr Oak House Hotel. This is the only childhood home of Laura that remains on its original site. You can tour the eleven-room restored hotel, an Advent Church built in 1877, and a 1910 bank building.

County Road A18 heads west over toward Route 139 where a left turn takes you on 139 south to rejoin Highway 9. Two miles west lies the small town of Cresco, known for its distinguished citizens and unique history. From the Spring of 1866 when it was first laid out to the Fall of that year, it grew into the most important town in Howard County, producing five admirals. A veteran's memorial has been placed in the courthouse square. Another well-known resident is Norman Borlaug who grew up on a farm outside of town and went on to win the 1970 Nobel Peace Prize for his contribution to agriculture. Borlaug is known as the founder of the Green Revolution. The town also was the home of Ellen Church, a war heroine, aviation pioneer, humanitarian, and the world's first airline stewardess.

A good place to start exploring Cresco is the Chamber of Commerce Welcome Center which also houses The Iowa Wrestling Hall of Fame. Here Iowa natives who have made significant contributions to amateur wrestling are honored.

The Howard County Historical Museum is located in the Kellow House, built by William Kellow Jr. in 1880.

The Heritage Train, a diesel locomotive built in LaGrange, Illinois in 1951, is also on display in Cresco. This was the first model sold to the Milwaukee Railroad Line.

Follow Route 9 south and east to Ridgeway, home to Beadle Park. A point of interest there is a log cabin which was continuously occupied for 110 years from 1854 to 1964. Except for the roof and downstairs floor, the cabin is completely original.

Turn south on CR W14 and head down to Spillville. Although tiny, with about 400 residents, Spillville has one of the most unusual combination museums in the country. The Bily Clock Museum houses many exquisite hand-carved clocks made in the early part of the 20th century by brothers Joseph and Frank Bily. Clocks range up to eight feet tall and weigh up to 500 pounds. Joseph designed the clocks, and Frank carved them. The American Pioneer History Clock took four years to complete and is considered the brothers' masterpiece.

On the second floor of the museum is an exhibit devoted to the famous Czech composer Antonin Dvorak. The Bily brothers collected Dvorak memorabilia after moving to the house where Dvorak spent the summer of 1893. Included in the collection are pump organs like those Dvorak used while writing his compositions. Behind the museum is the 1854 Bouska Schoolhouse Log Cabin.

Other points of interest in the town are St. Wenceslaus Church and cemetery. The church was built in 1860, and you can see the 1876 organ that Dvorak regularly played during his visit. You also will want to examine the unique crosses made by Charles Andera that adorn the cemetery.

You can take a break in Riverside Park on the banks of the Turkey River, a spot where Dvorak liked to sit and compose. The large Inwood Pavilion is also located in the park.

The Soldiers and Sailors Memorial Bandstand was built in the center of town as a memorial to the servicemen of World War I. A Polka Fest is held in the town in July.

A few miles south of Spillville you come to Fort Atkinson, a reconstructed military post built in the 1840s. Fort Atkinson is open to visitors any time during daylight hours; a museum gives the history of the post. The cannon house and the powder house are two particular points of interest. The fort became a state preserve in 1968. During the last full weekend in September, the Fort Atkinson Rendezvous is held to help educate the public about the role the fort played in the history of the area.

Take CR B32 east over to Festina and visit the St. Anthony of Padua Chapel, known as the world's smallest church. Inside the chapel, open during the daylight hours, is a beautiful altar and pews that seat just eight people. Also on the grounds is the 1849 log cabin that was the first home of Frank Joseph and Mary Ann (Gaertner) Huber, the couple credited with the building of the chapel. The church is kept up by descendents of the Huber and Gaertner families, and on the Sunday closest to June 13th the feast of St. Anthony of Padua mass is held on the tiny altar.

Leaving on 150 South to Eldorado, catch CR B40 and head east to Clermont where a wealth of historical sites is located in this small town on the banks of the Turkey River. In the second half of the nineteenth century brickmaking was a major industry, and this is reflected in the many fine brick buildings gracing the town. Clermont was so well known for its fine bricks that it earned the nickname "Brick City." Many of the buildings are listed on the National Register of Historic Places.

The best known of these structures is Montauk. This mansion, now a state preserve, was the home of William Larrabee, the twelfth governor of Iowa. Built of vintage brick and limestone in 1874, the house and grounds comprise forty-six acres and over one hundred thousand pine trees overlooking the Turkey River. Montauk was owned by the Larrabee family for over one hundred years and still has the original furnishings on display. It is now owned and administered by the State Historical Society of Iowa.

Another fascinating stop is the Riegel Blacksmith Shop. Burkard Riegel, a native of Germany and a master blacksmith from 1931 when he first came to Clermont until the early 1980s, operated the shop. A hallway has been constructed so that visitors can view the shop and all the original tools of the blacksmith trade.

Riegel shod not only farm and racehorses; he was also once called upon to shoe Gene Autry's famous horse

Champion before he could perform at the Fayette County Fair. Ornamental ironwork was another of Riegel's talents, and examples of his artistic wrought iron railings and decorative posts can be found in and around Clermont and points beyond.

The Clermont Opera House, started in 1911 and completed in 1912, was long the social center of the community and today is still used for community events, dances and plays. The original painted roll-up curtain is still in use.

The Larrabee School, donated to the city by Gov. and Mrs. Larrabee, now houses the city offices, the library, and Clermont Historical Museum. The Clermont Museum can be found in the 1913 Larrabee Bank which along with several other buildings is on the National Registry of Historic Places.

Two notable statues are located in the town. A statue of Abraham Lincoln is a duplicate of one that is in Edinburgh, Scotland. The second statue is of David B. Henderson, a Civil War hero who served for twenty years in the U.S. House of Representatives, the last four as Speaker of the House. He was the first speaker born west of the Mississippi.

From Clermont take Highway 18 north to Postville, a small town that takes pride in its cultural diversity. Residents trace their ethnic roots back to Jewish, Mexican, Russian, Ukrainian, Filipino, and Norwegian sources; many more cultures are represented in the town.

To learn more about this "Hometown to the World" and its beautiful natural surroundings you might like to stop at the Postville Visitors Center and then take a stroll through Diversity Garden.

From Postville you can take Route 51 north to Highway 9 or you can take a more circular route by taking County Roads B38 to where it connects with X16 north to Route 9 and back to Waukon. Or you can go a few miles east on Highway 18 and catch X16, a favorite motorcycling road, where it starts in Luana.

The scenic CR A52 takes you back east where you then turn left on X42 and follow that over to X52 just south of Lansing. This is a wonderful scenic ride which takes you through the Mississippi Bluff country and down to the village of Harper's Ferry.

In Harper's Ferry you can rest at the small park and decide if you wish to continue south on X52, a road sandwiched between high bluffs and the river, or go a couple of miles west and take a refreshing ride on B25 through the Yellow River State Forest. Primitive camping is available in the state forest at the Paint Creek and the Little Paint Creek Campgrounds. You really can't go wrong with either of these roads. Both connect with Route 76 heading south.

While on Route 76 you might want to stop at the Scenic Ridgeview Exotic Animal Ranch and pick up some buffalo meat, go for a hayrack ride, or visit the petting farm, which allows you to get up close and personal with several rare species. If you have ever wanted to try sleeping in a teepee you can plan to make this an overnight stop.

A bit farther south you come to Effigy Mounds National Monument which is the only National Park or Monument in Iowa. The prehistoric Indians used this area as a burial and ceremonial ground from around 500 B.C. to 1300 A.D. Except for the parking lot at the visitor's center, there are no roads at Effigy Mounds. The visitor's center has a museum, bookstore, historical displays, and rest rooms. A short film history of the mound builders is shown in the auditorium.

Effigy mounds are shaped into animal forms. There are four lookout points on the top of the bluff for those wanting to leave the bikes and get some exercise. It can be a stiff climb up the bluffs, but the views are a great reward. There is also hiking in the bottomland along the river.

In late September Effigy Mounds is the site of the annual Hawk Watch when enlightening educational and scientific programs are held throughout the weekend. Trained birdwatchers will help to identify the birds and answer questions about the annual hawk migrations. There is also a live raptor presentation featuring hawks and owls.

Three miles south of Effigy Mounds is the river town of Marquette. Marquette, along with its close river-town neighbor McGregor, form a district known as Mar-Mac.

The Isle of Capri gambling boat is located between the two towns. For more information on the area you can visit the Marquette Depot Museum, Gift Shop and Information Center. The museum gives a fascinating glimpse into the history of the area.

A look into frontier life can be found at the McGregor Historical Museum on Main Street in McGregor.

Pike's Peak State Park offers a fantastic view of the river where you get a different perspective on the confluence of the Mississippi and Wisconsin from the river's highest bluff. Looking straight across you will see Wyalusing State Park on the Wisconsin side of the river. Zebulon Pike mapped out the area in 1805 before he ever traveled west to Colorado and his more famous landmark. A hike along the boardwalk to Bridal Veil Falls will be worth your time. The park offers camping, hiking, and a chance to experience nature.

The pink elephant, long a landmark in Marquette, now stands near the entrance to the Isle of Capri.

County Road X56, an excellent road for bikers, heads south through the bluff country, and along the river to Guttenberg. In addition to the spectacular scenery, the 18-mile stretch contains a good number of twists and turns to help keep you alert.

Or you can take a longer loop ride to get to Guttenberg and along the way explore a cave, visit the world's first tractor, or enjoy several other interesting attractions.

A relaxed method of cave exploration can be found at Spook Cave seven miles west of McGregor on Highways 18 and 52. There is no walking in the cave; however, an interesting thirty-five minute guided tour is conducted by boat. This is not a good place for those with claustrophobia since there are places where the roof of the cave is very low, and you have to duck down into the boat to avoid a concussion. The cave opens for visitors on weekends beginning in late April and remains open through the end of October.

The site was originally called Spook Hole by the early settlers who were startled by the strange sounds issuing from the hole at the bottom of a hill along Bloody Run Creek. It took Gerald Mielke to finally track down the source of the sounds. In 1953 Mielke blasted a hole wide enough to pass through and discovered the cave and an underground river. He built a lock and dam to control the water level in the cave. After the cave was opened, the strange noises ceased. According to geologists, the changing water levels roaring through the narrow passages made the sounds, or you can accept the local legend that Mielke released the spirits that had been trapped underground.

Heading west on Highway 18 you will find Froelich, a historical village where in 1892 John Froelich invented the first gasoline engine that could be driven both forward and backward. This engine would eventually replace the heavy steam engines that were, in that age, used to power farm machinery. A scale model of the Froelich tractor, which was the forerunner of the John Deere tractor, is housed in the general store. A replica also is exhibited in the blacksmith shop.

Froelich was a prolific inventor and is credited with developing the washing machine, dishwasher, and dryer, as well as a mechanical corn picker, and he was the first to mount a gasoline engine on a well drilling outfit. He also invented the first air conditioner. The company he founded eventually became the Carrier Air Conditioning Company.

The village currently is being restored to reflect life in the 1800s. During the last weekend in September, the village holds the "Fall-der-all" featuring tractors from the original Froelich model to the latest John Deere models on display.

About a mile south of Froelich on Highway 52 you can turn off on Route 13 and wind your way south to Elkader.

Nine structures in Elkader, including the 1888 Keystone Bridge, are listed on the National Registry of Historic Places. The Carter House Museum is one of the Midwest's finest examples of Greek Revival architecture and houses a display of antique furniture and historical artifacts. Live entertainment is provided at the Elkader Opera House by the Opera House Players, and the opera house also attracts a variety of local and national entertainers throughout the year.

A scenic walk along the Turkey River takes you from downtown to the city park which features sixty to seventy campsites, with electrical hook-ups and a convenient bathhouse with hot showers.

Adjacent to the park is the George Maier Rural Heritage Center. The rebuilt Elkader Sales Barn houses a portion of the George Maier's extensive collection of articles from the rural history of Iowa.

Another interesting stop is the Big Springs Trout Hatchery. Rainbow, Brook and Brown Trout are raised to stockable size in the twenty-four spring-fed raceways and four earthen ponds and then released to twenty-one streams in northeast Iowa. Water is supplied by Big Springs Iowa's largest spring. The hatchery is located on Big Springs Road, ten miles west of Elkader.

Five miles south of Elkader on Highway 13 you will want to stop at the Osborne Visitor Welcome and Nature Center. You'll find a comfortable rest stop, helpful travel information, a gift shop featuring unique Iowa products, and educational wildlife and conservation displays. A pioneer village, arboretum, a live animal exhibit, and several outdoor recreation facilities and hiking trails are on the grounds.

The Motor Mill Historic Site five miles southeast of Elkader along the Turkey River includes a six-story limestone mill and several outbuildings including an inn, a stable, an ice house, and a cooperage. The village of Motor occupied the site from the 1840s to the 1870s.

From here you can turn off on CR X3C and take it over to CR C7X or continue south on Highway 13 to Strawberry Point, home of the World's Largest Strawberry. Standing fifteen feet high and twelve feet across, it would make a huge strawberry shortcake. Also in Strawberry Point you will find the Wilder Memorial Museum. Here you can step back in time and view over 800 heirloom dolls; a collection of Victorian lamps including one from the movie *Gone With the Wind*; and displays of rare European figurines, exquisite glass and porcelain, toy farm tractors, and pioneer tools.

Three miles south is Backbone State Park; dedicated in 1920, this was the first state park in Iowa. This area consists of steep rugged terrain cut by a loop in the Maquoketa River. If you want some adventurous exercise, the steep cliffs are very popular with climbers and rappellers. For over one hundred years this high rocky ridge was known as the Devil's Backbone, which was shortened to give the park its unusual name.

From Backbone head north back up to Highway 3 and over to Edgewood, the site of Bixby State Preserve, a nature lover's dream spot. There you can find a delicate micro-ecosystem formed by moist air coming from an ice cave. The preserve also features a trout stream and two challenging hiking trails. One trail leads up to Steamboat Rock and the other up to Castle Rock. The bird's eye view from the top of Castle Rock is worth the effort.

The town of Edgewood is located in two counties with Highway 3 as the border between them. Those living north of the highway are in Clayton County, while those to the south are in Delaware County. The annual Rodeo Days are held in Edgewood in late June.

Continuing east you can follow Highway 3, which is a nice ride, or turn north on CR C7X. This road is a favorite of bikers and has a few nice sweepers, a couple of hills, and a scenic ride along the top of a ridge. At the end of C7X, you will be back to the river and the town of Guttenberg.

An alluring riverside park stretches for a mile along the length of Guttenberg. You can stop for a rest, eat a picnic lunch, and watch the boats and barges heading up and down the river. The town has several well-preserved limestone buildings listed on the National Register of Historic Places, and a walking tour of the town will give you a chance to shop or eat in many of them.

In 1934 Rudolph Wolter built a monument in the Riverside Park honoring the area's Native Americans.

You might also wish to visit the State Fish Aquarium and Hatchery and view some of the fish native to the Mississippi and several species of trout from nearby streams. An exhibit of buttons made in Guttenberg from Mississippi River shells also can be found here.

The Lockmaster's House Heritage Museum provides a look into Guttenberg history. This is the only surviving lockmaster house on the Upper Mississippi River and is part of the lock and dam system owned by the Army Corps of Engineers. Just outside is an observation platform which allows you to watch the barges lock through Lock and Dam #10.

During the fourth weekend in September the town celebrates its ethnic heritage with the annual German Fest which includes German music featuring Guttenberg's German band, a beer garden, arts and crafts vendors, and German food at the local restaurants.

Just south of town on Highway 52 an overlook provides a panoramic view of the town and river.

Continue South on Route 52 to Millville, where you definitely will want to turn off onto CR C9Y. Just outside of town a gravel road takes you to the car ferry across the river to Cassville, Wisconsin, but you won't want to miss the ride farther along C9Y. Winding along a high ridge, the road gives wonderful views of the countryside and glimpses of the river in the distance. This road is a great favorite with motorcyclists in Northeastern Iowa.

About halfway along you will come to the tiny hamlet of Balltown, population debatable but under fifty. However the magnet that draws people to Balltown is the famous Breitbach's Restaurant. This is the oldest continuously operating bar and restaurant in Iowa, serving the public since 1852. The Breitbach family has owned the restaurant since 1891, and current owner Mike Breitbach is the fifth generation to keep up the family tradition of great home-cooked food.

The mural of the countryside is a focal point of the bar at Breitbach's Country Dining.

A homelike atmosphere and sense of history engulf you as soon as you enter the building. On the wall in the back of the bar is an exquisite mural of the surrounding countryside. The story is that during the depression, a band of hungry and destitute gypsies wandered into Balltown. Alberto, one member of the group, was a skilled painter, so in return for food and a couple of weeks' shelter, he offered to paint the lovely mural. The mural was "lost" and forgotten behind paneling for several years but was re-discovered a few years ago when the paneling was removed during refurbishing. Recognizing the beauty of the work, Mike had the mural cleaned, and it now once more stands as a focal point of the bar.

Outside of the restaurant a short walk takes you to one of the most breathtaking views of the valley. From the overlook you will see several farms and the ribbon of Mississippi, and (if the day is clear) sharp-eyed viewers can spot the giant M on the bluff at Platteville, Wisconsin.

Groaning from the meal at Breitbach's, you climb back on the bikes and roar out of Balltown on C9Y for the scenic ride to Sageville, just outside of the city of Dubuque.

The three-state view from the overlook in Balltown is stunning.

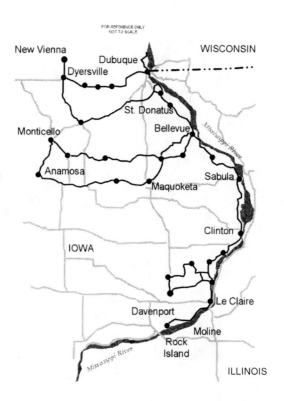

Returning along the river in Iowa

CHAPTER NINE

DUBUQUE TO THE QUAD CITIES

A leisurely trip back to your starting point in the Quad Cities will give you an opportunity to leave the bike and ride the world's steepest cable car, enjoy the lovely waterfront parks stretching through picturesque villages, thrill to the sight of majestic riverboats, and then tackle a huge three-quarter pound hamburger. You will experience a bit of the Wild West by visiting the boyhood home and the museum of Buffalo Bill Cody, and (if you still have the strength) you can end up partying at the largest motorcycle rally in the Midwest.

The Eagle Point district is located on the north side of Dubuque and contains the large Eagle Point City Park which overflows with picnic areas, native stone shelters, and overlooks of the river. Lock and Dam #11 is directly below the park; an overhead lookout point gives you an eagle's-eye view of the barges and pleasure boats as they lock through.

There is a great deal to see and do in Dubuque. West of the Eagle Point district is the sprawling College Grandview District, the location of several colleges and the University of Dubuque. This district also contains the Dubuque Arboretum and Botanical Gardens in Marshall Park. Among the attractions in the arboretum are award-winning all-American rose gardens, native plants and grasses, a dwarf conifer collection, and the nation's largest Hosta glade.

The Port of Dubuque is a hotbed of activity. On an island below the north bridge that crosses over into Wisconsin is the Dubuque Greyhound Park and Casino, and on the south end of the island is McAleece Park and Recreation Complex.

A tugboat, pushing its barges, enters the gates of Lock and Dam #11 in Dubuque, Iowa.

The latest showcase of the Port is the National Mississippi River Museum and Aquarium. A full day could be spent wandering around the many exhibits including fresh water aquariums, working riverboats, a wetland nature trail, living history presentations, and noteworthy displays celebrating the history of the Mississippi.

If you want some gambling action and don't want to go to the dogs there is the Diamond Jo Riverboat Casino. Another site on the waterfront is the shot tower, which pays tribute to the town's past as a producer of munitions.

You can chose among several methods to explore the historic downtown area. Besides walking tours, there are carriage rides, trolleys, and mini vans. River rides are provided by the nostalgic riverboat the Spirit of Dubuque or the sleek and modern Miss Dubuque.

No trip to Dubuque would be complete without a ride on the Fenelon Place Elevator, the world's shortest and steepest scenic railway. The spectacular view from the platform at the top of the elevator includes three states, the city, and the port.

The two cars of the Fenelon Place Elevator pass as they head up and down the steep railway.

The arts certainly have not been overlooked in

Dubuque. Live theater productions are mounted in the recently-renovated 1889 Grand Opera House. The Five Flags Civic Center was modeled after the Moulin Rouge in Paris and was built in 1910. It covers a full city block and is home to the Five Flags Theater which hosts the Dubuque Symphony Orchestra. An extensive Grant Wood collection is featured in the Dubuque Museum of Art. The town also boasts several Victorian homes from the early days of Dubuque. Food and lodging of all types are plentiful in the city.

On the south side of Dubuque is the Mines of Spain recreation area which contains the grave and monument to city founder Julian Dubuque. The main headquarters of Wilwert's Harley Davidson/Buell is located just off Route 22 on North Crescent Ridge.

NASCAR series stockcar racing is held on Sunday nights at the Dubuque County Fairgrounds off of Route 20 on the western edge of the city.

Traveling west on Highway 20 you will come to a second area speedway at the small town of Farley which hosts NASCAR series racing on Friday evenings.

A few miles further on Route 20 you will come to Dyersville, and movie buffs will recognize this town as the site of the *Fields of Dreams*. This field is a major tourist attraction for movie fans and baseball fans alike. Admission to the site is free and visitors can run bases, bat balls, or sit on the bleachers and wait for the ghostly visitors to arrive. Care must be taken however, since the field sits on two different farms and one side closes earlier in the evening than the other.

Also in Dyersville is the National Farm Toy Museum where you will find over 30,000 farm toys exhibited at the museum along with a theater and gift shop. A tourist information center is located next to the museum.

For those interested in antiques, over 150 dealers

stock the 22,500 square feet of the Plaza Antique Mall.

A collection of over 1000 dolls is on display at the Dyer-Botsford Doll Museum in the Victorian home of Dyersville's founder, as well as a rare German feather Christmas tree, a replica of an 1850 castle, and a hand-carved miniature circus.

One of the finest examples of Gothic architecture in the Midwest can be found at the Basilica of St. Francis Xavier, one of only fifty-two basilicas in the United States. The basilica has 212-foot twin spires and sixty-four stained glass windows.

Four miles northeast of Dyersville is the Becker Woodcarving Museum where many forms of woodcarving are exhibited and demonstrated. You can watch the ongoing work of carving a full-size carousel, marvel at Iowa's largest carved clock, and examine a collection of Native American artifacts.

Three Riverboats can be seen docked at the port from the platform at the top of Fenelon Place Elevator.

A short side trip takes you north to where the

Heritage House Museum is located in the town of New Vienna. A former convent, it has been converted to a German museum. There are twenty-three rooms filled with antiques, artifact, and handmade quilts, and the entrance and staircase feature pressed tin walls and ceilings.

From New Vienna take Highway 136 south to Route 151 and then turn northeast to CR D41 and head east over to Highway 52 and back to the Great River Road.

A turn to the south takes you Iowa's largest show cave, Crystal Lake Cave. While exploring the cave's three-quarter-mile length, you will see an incredible display of rare and beautiful formations. Crystal Lake Cave is one of only two known caves in the United States that has a formation known as Anthodites, familiarly known as cave flowers. Other fantastic formations include St. Peter's Dome, the Chandelier, the Chapel, and the Pipe Organ. Tons of brown onyx can be seen in many of the passageways.

Movie buffs can look for the sign announcing the entrance to the Field of Dreams *movie site.*

The underground lake, from which the cave gets its name, is water filtered by seepage through the rocks into its purest form. Cave temperature is a constant fifty degrees so wearing a light jacket or sweater is advised.

Continuing south on Route 52 brings you to the Historic Luxembourg Village of St. Donatus. Two huge churches dominate the first view of the town. To the south along the highway is the German Lutheran St. John's Church and nestled at the bottom of a hill on the edge of town is St. Donatus Catholic Church.

Behind the Catholic Church you will find the Stations of the Cross winding up Cavalry Hill to the Pieta Chapel. This outdoor Way of the Cross was the first in North America and was constructed in 1861. The Pieta Chapel, dedicated to the Virgin Mary was added in 1865.

The Gehlen House Bed and Breakfast was built in the Quereinhaus style popular in Luxembourg where the house and barn are combined under one roof and occupies the native stone home built in 1847 by Peter Gehlen, an immigrant from Luxembourg. The house was given a facelift in 1997 by a group of artisans and builders who traveled from Luxembourg to complete the job.

A good place to stop for some genuine Luxembourg cuisine is Kalmes Restaurant. For forty-three years the Kalmes family has served a special sausage made from a recipe brought from Luxembourg in 1840 by Peter Kalmes. Don't miss the massive bar that also came from Luxembourg at the same time. The village also has a Kalmes General Store. The ethnic heritage of the village is celebrated in June during Luxembourg Days.

Once more head south on Route 52 to the town of Bellevue, the only town along the river named for its beautiful view and one of the five oldest towns in Iowa. An enchanting riverside park stretches along the entire length of the town, and there also are many spots to stop and rest and enjoy a picnic lunch or just sit and watch the boats on the river. This includes a newly-built, Rotary-sponsored overlook platform, complete with several benches.

The first Station of the Cross is visible behind the lovely St. Donatus Catholic Church.

The main part of town has many historic homes and businesses, with many of the buildings having been constructed of native limestone. Hungry bikers can opt for fast food or perhaps sample the good home cooking at Richman's Café. One of the best-known structures is Potter's Mill, built in 1843. The mill was in operation until 1969, making good use of the terraced rapids on Mill Creek. It has since been renovated and now houses a full service restaurant and a Bed & Breakfast.

Over 160 years old, Potter's Mill in Bellevue has been turned into a unique restaurant and Bed & Breakfast.

Other vintage buildings include a hexagonal barn built in 1921 and Mont Rest, the home built by wealthy Bellevue native Seth Baker. Mont Rest is known locally as "the castle," given its lofty site looking down on the village. It is now a luxurious bed and breakfast.

Bellevue State Park consists of two units. The Nelson Unit, located at the south edge of the village gives magnificent views of the town, river, and Lock & Dam #12 from the lookout points. This area also contains the South Bluff Nature Center which features displays of the geology, plant, and animals native to the area. The Garden Sanctuary for Butterflies is the only one of its kind in the Midwest. Over 100 plots planted to provide food and habitat for a wide variety of these beautiful insects are among the walking paths, and a small pond dominates the center of the sanctuary.

The Dyas Unit, two miles south on 52, has seven miles of foot trails. There is also a gravel road leading to it. You will find a self guided nature trail, scenic overlooks, and a stream with beaver dams, along with various aquatic and other wildlife. There is also a wonderful variety of wildflowers.

Bellevue is the eastern edge of the Grant Wood Scenic Byway that will provide a side trip you won't want to miss. Route 62 will take you southwest through the beautiful hill country.

Fourteen miles from Bellevue is the village of Andrew nestled at the foot of the bluffs. Just to the north of the town is the Andrew Jackson Demonstration Farm on the site of the former County Home. Here on the 360-acre site those with an interest in agriculture can learn different tillage methods and discover a new wheat-rye cover crop called triticale.

You might want to stop for a rest in the Andrew City Park located in the center of town; located in the park is the 120-year-old Andrew Jail Historical Site. This three-story limestone structure includes cell room, the exercise yard, jailer's quarters, the prison kitchen, and the sheriff's office. Tours are by appointment. Andrew also is the birthplace of Ansel Briggs, Iowa's first governor.

Six miles beyond Andrew is the town of Maquoketa, the county seat of Jackson County. This small community offers unusual scenic and cultural opportunities for visitors.

The Old City Hall Gallery was originally built in 1901 as a fire station and then became the city hall and police station and has now been transformed into an art gallery. Original oil paintings by nationally-known realistic impressionist artist Rose Frantzen are exhibited. Also on display are antiques, sculpture, pottery and scenic photography of Jackson County. The wildlife artwork of Patrick J. Costello is featured at Costello's Old Mill Gallery, located in a refurbished old grist mill.

There is also a community theater group.

The Jackson County Fairgrounds is home to the Jackson County Historical Society Museum. The county heritage; antique farm machinery, including horse drawn implements; and many rotating exhibits and traveling displays can be found at the museum.

The city boasts ten parks plus the restored Huntsville Limestone Kilns. At one time the kilns provided 1000 barrels of fine lime per day. The Huntsville Interpretive Center along Highway 61 offers several displays and programs to help people understand the history and operation of the kilns. Before leaving Maquoketa you also might want to check out Kleppe's Power Sports home to Kawasaki and Suzuki sales and service. They also carry a full line of biker gear and accessories.

Four miles west of the town is Maquoketa Caves State Park. At the park you can stretch your legs by exploring some of the thirteen limestone caves, visiting the natural bridge, or enjoying viewing the many unusual rock formations. For those who do not feel like exploring the rugged terrain of the park the geology and history of the early inhabitants can be found at the recently restored visitors' center.

From Maquoketa bikers will want to head west on Route 64 about thirty-five miles to Anamosa. On the way you might want to stop in the hamlet of Baldwin and visit the Mill Rock Schoolhouse, a limestone school restored and maintained by the Jackson County Conservation Board. Also near Baldwin is the Eden Valley Nature Center, where you will find picnicking, fishing, and camping facilities along with nature lectures by a DNR Board staff member.

Providing a haven for a wide variety of waterfowl, Baldwin Marsh is a twenty-acre fresh water project administered by the Jackson County

Conservation Board. The marsh is also the home of an endangered species of orchid.

You can stop and sample the wines at Tabor Home Vineyards and watch the vineyard activities and the winemaking process.

Two miles farther along Route 64 you can find several opportunities for agri-tourism at the village of Monmouth. Tractor buffs can visit the acres of antique tractors at the Frantzen Family Used Tractor and Parts, the areas largest salvage tractor yard. During the summer, horse-drawn wagon rides are available at 4-D-Acres. Picnic and camping grounds and an enclosed shelter are also on site. During the winter months, you can enjoy a ride in a horsedrawn bobsled. You can also see high stepping Hackney ponies pulling sulkies at the Gib Marcucci Stables or simply stop for a rest in the city park.

The Wyoming Historical Museum in the town of Wyoming has a display of old pharmaceutical items, an old-fashioned ice cram parlor and a craft shop. There are plans to expand the exhibits in the museum.

Four miles from Anamosa beside Highway 64 you will find the Grant Wood Memorial Park. In the park is Antioch School where the famous artist began his education. The school is on the National Registry of Historic Places. Also in the park is a building embellished with a replica of Wood's well known painting of a farm couple entitled "American Gothic."

In Anamosa, make your first stop downtown at the National Motorcycle Museum and Hall of Fame. A full history of the sport can be found here along with a constantly changing and expanded collection of antique and famous bikes. Fans of the 1960's movie *Easy Rider* can find the only Captain America bike in existence which has been authenticated and signed by Peter Fonda. Another exhibit details the exploits of Evel Knievel.

Bikes on display range from the earliest 1880 models to the latest present-day models.

Antioch School, the first school attended by renowned Iowa artist Grant Wood.

The Hall of Fame honors those men and women in the categories of competition, industry, leadership, and promotion who have influenced the sport of motorcycling. Allow yourself plenty of time to see all the fascinating exhibits.

For a change of pace you can then visit the Anamosa State Penitentiary Museum. You will learn the 132-year history of Iowa's largest prison and can visit the gift shop for prison memorabilia. The museum is open Friday, Saturday and Sunday from Memorial Day to October from noon to 4:00 p.m.

Grant Wood enthusiasts can find a history of the artist along with gifts, prints, posters, and note cards at the Grant Wood Art Gallery in downtown Anamosa. For more Grant Wood history you might also want to journey a few miles west along CR E28 to Stone City for the Grant Wood Art Festival held the second Sunday in June.

The Ryan Norlin Pumpkin Weigh-Off is highlighted the first weekend in October during the annual Pumpkinfest. Pumpkins weighing over 1000 pounds have been entered in the competition, and a parade, pumpkin carving exhibitions, pumpkin recipe contest, and many more fun activities are on the schedule of this autumn event.

The beautiful Sturgis Fiftieth Anniversary Bike is on exhibit at the National Motorcycle Museum and Hall of Fame in Anamosa, Iowa.

On the north side of Anamosa on Route 151 you will find J&P Cycles, a must-stop for anyone looking for aftermarket parts and accessories. In addition to putting out their large mail-order catalog, the company also sponsors the Annual J&P Poker Run for Camp Courageous in mid June and J&P Cycles Customer Appreciation Day in late June.

Follow Route 151 north to the town of Monticello

where just north of town is the lovely Riverside Gardens, a city park built and maintained strictly by volunteers. The thirteen acres of gardens allow you to wander through thirty-eight flower beds, a wetland and prairie nature preserve, a gift shop, and a nature center.

There are also several other parks in and around the town, along with a state-of-the-art aquatic center, and the town boasts two historic bridges. The Bowstring Bridge in Central Park was constructed in 1873 and crossed the Maquoketa River on historic Military Road and was moved to the park in 1985. The triple arch stone bridge was built out of native stone in 1862 and is still in use today. Monticello is also the home of Camp Courageous, a recreation and respite care facility for persons with disabilities.

Three miles south of Monticello and two miles east of Route 38 you can visit Pictured Rock Park where you will find a scenic tour between the cliffs of the Maquoketa River. Trails and caves invite you take a bit of time and do some exploring.

Another three miles south on 38 you will find CR E17 at the town of Scotch Grove site of Edinburgh Ghost Town and Museum. Twelve historical buildings including a log cabin, school house, church, depot, and blacksmith shop are on display.

Turn east and E17 will take you through the farms and hills back over to Highway 52.

As a part of the Great River Road, Highway 52 winds its way south through the bluff country to the island city of Sabula. The only community in Iowa located on an island, Sabula is a wonderful place for fishermen. The South Sabula Lakes Park allows you to camp or picnic right on the edge of the water. Heading east on Highways 52 and 64 you follow a narrow ribbon of highway flanked on both sides by water. The bridge takes you over into Illinois at Savanna. Heading west and south you will want to stop at the Jackson County Welcome Center. Housed in a replica of a an old fashioned school house you will find a wealth of information on Eastern Iowa, clean rest rooms, a gift shop featuring country crafts and a warm welcome from the friendly staff.

The Great River Road (now Highway 67) winds its way through the bluff country south for about six miles to Andover Road where a right turn will take you to Almont Tap where a sign in front says "fun in a cornfield." This stop is a favorite with hungry bikers, who wait all day to tackle the "specialty of the house," the famous three-quarter pound hamburger. Served with fries, this monster burger will satisfy a king-sized appetite.

One of the most picturesque Welcome Centers in Iowa is the replica of an old-fashioned schoolhouse outside of Sabula.

This is not fast food. The burgers are cooked when they are ordered, but you don't mind the wait once you taste one of these delicacies. For those who aren't up to tackling such a big meal, there are also other items on the menu.

Stuffed and groaning as you leave the Almont Tap, mount the bike for a six-mile scenic ride south to Clinton. Just north of the city turn left and visit Clinton's Eagle Point City Park. This beautifully-landscaped 200-acre park provides a twisting ride along the cliffs, stunning vistas of the widest part of the river, and even a stone tower giving a panoramic view of the area from the turrets.

The rustic Eagle Point Lodge, with a glassed-in fireplace and spectacular river views, may be rented for special occasions.

The third weekend in May the park hosts the annual Civil War Re-Enactment weekend, with appearances by President Lincoln, tours of the army camps, an old-fashioned barn dance, and a full-scale battle.

Just to the south of the park entrance is the Soaring Eagle Nature Center. This includes educational displays, natural prairie, wetlands area, hiking trails, and a petting farm. All exhibits are free to the public.

There are many sites and activities to enjoy in Clinton. You will definitely want to ride along the levee that includes the spectacular Riverfront Park. There are ample places to stop and rest or picnic and watch the boats and barges. Also along the levee is the Mississippi Belle II Riverboat Casino and the Clinton Area Showboat Theater. A professional summer repertory company mounts great productions from June through mid-August.

Other events held at Riverview Park are Art in the Park on the Saturday before Father's Day, and Riverboat Days, the area's largest Fourth of July Celebration which actually spans several days. The second Sunday in August the Riverfront is the site of the

Rod & Custom Car Show featuring over 150 vehicles.

Sports fans will want to visit Alliant Energy Field and root for the Clinton Lumber Kings, a Class A baseball team affiliated with the Texas Rangers. The color and spectacle of masses of hot air balloons rising at one time is showcased at Balloons in June. The night ascent of glowing balloons is a breathtaking sight you won't want to miss.

Jeff Alls and Jody Nelson rest beside a stone wall to enjoy the view of the river

The Felix Adler Discovery Center is a hands-on museum honoring Clinton native Frank (Felix) Adler, the king of clowns who spent almost fifty years with the Ringling Brothers and Barnum & Bailey Circus.

The Riverboat Celebration Belle passes Riverview Park in Clinton on her way upriver.

Other interesting stops include Bickellhaupt Arboretum, a fourteen-acre outdoor museum featuring one of the finest dwarf and rare conifer collections in the country. Included are over 600 cultivars, flowers, and other plants. A museum exhibit of native animals and birds is also on the site.

The history of Clinton and the story of the early settlers and lumber barons is on display at the Historical Society Museum. Of particular interest is the "Resolute," one of only three manually-powered fire engines in the world.

Clinton is one of the smallest cities to host a full, professional symphony orchestra, and the Gateway Contemporary Ballet Company has been performing classical and modern dance for over fifteen years. The River Arts Center presents exhibits in a wide variety of media, and the gift shop contains the work of many area artists. For bikers in need of Genuine Harley parts, accessories, or clothing you might want to check out Clinton Harley Davidson at 2519 Lincolnway. They also have an excellent service department.

Just south of Clinton on Route 67 is the town of Camanche. Unlike the Indian tribe, the name of the town is pronounced "Com Manch." The Camanche Depot & Museum sits on the grounds and consists of a restored 1899 depot and a 1951 Milwaukee/Soo Line Caboose. You can also explore the ecology of the river by taking a Blue Heron Eco Cruise offered by the Clinton County Conservation Board. Each educational cruise lasts about one and a half hours. During the second full weekend in August, the town celebrates Camanche Days with a carnival, parade, and various sporting contests.

Route 67 continues south to just north of Princeton where you turn off on CR F33 and follow the signs to visit the Cody Homestead. This was the boyhood home of the famous scout and showman Buffalo Bill Cody. In 1847 Isaac Cody, father to Buffalo Bill, built the house out of native limestone. The house has been restored and features much vintage furniture. You will find buffalo and longhorn cattle grazing in the pastures surrounding the home.

More signs will lead you through the countryside to Dan Nagle's Walnut Grove Pioneer Village. Eighteen historical buildings populate the village. In the 1860's Walnut Grove was a crossroads community and stagecoach stop. As it has been for several generations, Old St. Ann's Church in the village is the site for many non-denominational weddings throughout the year.

The village is located at the north end of Scott County Park, a 1280-acre park offering a variety of outdoor activities, with an Olympic-size swimming pool providing a great place to stop and cool off on a hot day.

Cody Homestead outside of Princeton Iowa was the boyhood home of Buffalo Bill.

Two miles to the west is the town of Long Grove where you will find the Alexander Brownlie Sod Home. This 1838 authentic sod house is on the National Register of Historic Places. From Long Grove take CR Y64 south to CR F45 and follow it back east to Princeton. The park along the river makes a nice place to stop for a rest or a picnic. Excellent chicken is available at Bridge's Waterfront, hard to miss with the huge chicken on the roof. Kernan's Riverview Restaurant is another great place to enjoy a meal while you sit and watch the river in comfort.

Route 67 follows closely along the river to the town of LeClaire which marks the Iowa site for the Great River Tug Fest. The rivalry with the Illinois residents across the river in Port Byron is always intense. LeClaire is also famous as the home to many river pilots. These men built fine homes mostly between 1850 and 1870. A self-guided tour will take you past these houses although they are still private dwellings and not open to the public.

Another piece of history is available at the

Buffalo Bill Museum which chronicles the life of the legendary figure, who was born in LeClaire. In addition to Buffalo Bill and Annie Oakley, the museum is also a memorial to the steamboat and pioneer history.

A favorite stop for bikers in LeClaire is Sneaky Pete's, a restaurant with a couple of unique differences: the salad bar is in a bathtub filled with ice, and anyone who enters wearing a necktie faces having it cut off and hung from the ceiling.

A visit to the Mississippi Valley Welcome Center just off of Interstate 80 at the south side of LeClaire will provide a wealth of information on the area along with a wonderful view of the river.

This replica of the famous riverboat "Robert E. Lee" is on display at the Buffalo Bill Museum in LeClaire.

LeClaire is located just at the north edge of the Quad Cities area and takes us back to our starting place.

The Quad Cities consists of Davenport and Bettendorf in Iowa and Moline and Rock Island in

Illinois. The river divides these four cities and several smaller outlaying communities. There is much to see and do with events taking place every weekend.

In addition to the beauty of its physical location at the bend of the river, some of the more-well known attractions include The Putnam Museum and Imax Theater, the River Center and Adler Theater on the Iowa side, and the Mark of Quad Cities in Moline. The District in Rock Island is also a hotbed of activity or you can try your luck at one of the Riverboat Casinos that are located in both states.

A short time exploring nature on the trails at Blackhawk State Park in Rock Island will be a nice bonus along with a visit to the fascinating museum, with its history exhibits and Native American lore, also located in the park.

I'm not going to dwell on all the attractions in the Quad Cities area, but I will mention one event that is of particular interest to bikers. "Sturgis on the River" is the largest motorcycle rally in the Midwest and is held in mid-June at the showgrounds west of Centennial Bridge and LeClaire Park in Davenport, Iowa. This three-day gathering is for anyone who loves motorcycles, fun runs, music, and a good time.

There are numerous bike shops throughout the Quad Cities, and bikes of almost any brand can find a dealership servicing their favorite. Some of the better known stores are Wiebler's Quad City Harley Davidson, in Davenport, Hawkeye Motor Works dealing in Honda's also in Davenport and Brenny's Motorcycle Clinics, selling Yamaha, Suzuki and Kawasaki in Bettendorf. Brenney's Cycle Works is located on the Illinois side of the river in Silvis. Also in Illinois is Hobart's Cycle and Tri City Motorcycle Sales in Rock Island and Fun Mart Cycle Center in Moline.

One other famous event is held each year at the

end of July each year in Davenport. Jazz lovers will not want to miss the Bix Beiderbecke Memorial Jazz Festival. The Festival and Bix 7K run draws jazz fans and runners from around the world for the weekend of music and partying on the riverfront.

In closing, an old folk song says, "Something is Always Happening on the River," and that is very true of the Mississippi. If you are looking for a large motorcycle rally or wish to take a fascinating look into history; if you'd like to visit some quaint small towns, sample some great food, enjoy a variety of celebrations and festivals; or if you simply want to ride some scenic and challenging roads, you will find what you are looking for in the Upper Mississippi Valley.

Appendix I
Trip Log

Chapter 1: The River Towns

Day/ Date	Location	Road	Mile	Rating	Note
Tues. 6/8/04	Erie	Moline Rd	0	**	Heading over to the river. Sky overcast.
	Campbell's Island to Albany	Rt. 84	49	***	Stopped in Albany for a break.
	Back to Erie	Back roads	62	**	Heading out again, sky cleared.
	Prophetstown	Back roads	74		Rode through park.
	Deer Grove	Hahnaman Rd	91	**	Tried an elk brat at elk farm.
	Grand Detour	Rt. 2	122	****	Stopped at John Deere Home & Museum.
	Rockford	R2	154	****	Lovely ride along Rock River.
	Oregon	33	176	***	Stop at Indian Statue.
	Polo	Pines Rd	190	*	Almost wiped out in Water Crossing at White Pines St. Park.
	Mt. Carroll	Rt. 52	215	**	Stopped for a rest at Timber Lake.
	Savanna	Rt. 84	226	***	Rode through Palisades St. Park. Awesome overlooks.
	Thomson	""	235	***	Picked up fresh produce, open air market.
	Fulton	""	242	**	Can't stop - clouding up again
	Erie	Diamond and Albany Rds	260	**	Started raining just before Erie.

Chapter 2: Hills and Curves at the Top of Illinois

Day/ Date	Location	Road	Mile	Rating	Note
Wed. 6/23/04	Erie, IL	Moline Rd.	0	**	Beautiful day for a ride.
	Mt. Carroll	78N	36	***	Stopped for break at square, then continued north.
	Scenic Ridge Rd	" "	38	****	Turned off into the hills.
	Derinda Rd	" "	52	*****	Most beautiful ride in Illinois.
	Elizabeth	" "	62	****	Enjoyed Terrapin Ridge. Visited Apple River Fort
	Tower on Rt. 20	Back roads to Rt. 20	64	*****	Climbed tower, spectacular views from all directions. Well maintained modern rest rooms
	Chestnut Mt. Resort	Blackjack Rd	74	****	Rode ski lift down and up the bluff. Fun!
	Galena	Rt. 20	83	****	Stopped for lunch.
	Lena	Stage-coach Trail	121	****	Circled Lake Le-Aqua-Na State park.
	Winslow	Rt.	130	***	Filled water bottles at artesian well.
	Morrison	Various back roads to 78	260	*****	Spectacular rides through the hills.
	Erie	Back roads	310	***	Got home and collapsed

Chapter 3: Wisconsin Wonderland

Day/ Date	Location	Road	Mile	Rating	Note
Fri. 7/9/04	Erie	Moline Rd	0	*	Warm humid day.
	Elizabeth	Back roads	60	*****	Always willing to travel this gorgeous country.
	Scales Md	Scales Md Road	73	******	The second prettiest road in Illinois. Highest altitude in state.
	Shullsburg, WI	CR O	86	***	Took a break, visited Gravity Hill.
	Mineral Point	CR O	110	****	Lots of hills. Halfway along got incredible close-up picture of a Red Tail Hawk. Tried a Cornish Pasty for lunch.
	New Glarus	39	141	**	Visited historic Swiss village.
	Monroe	CR N	156	*	Stayed the night in Monroe.
Sat. 7/10/04	Argyll	81	25	***	Circled Yellowstone Lake.
	Gratiot	78	40	****	Nice sweeps on this section of 78.
	New Diggings	CR W	60	****	South on 78 to west and then turn east. Macho burger at Antons.
	Hazel Green	CR W& Rt. 11	65	****	Continue east on 11.
	Sinsinawa Mound	CR Z	72	****	A must stop to buy bread.
	Dickeyville	CR HH	82	***	Visited the Grotto.
	Tennyson/ Potosi	Rt. 35	90	****	Break at Grant River Rec. Area.
	Cassville	133	119	****	Visited Stonefield Village

	Wyalusing State Park	Several CRs	145	*****	Wild country, hairpin curves, gorgeous scenery.
	Fennimore	61	170	***	Starting back south.
	Erie, IL	Moline Rd	308	**	Home late, completely worn out.

Chapter 4: Ride the Lower Wisconsin River

Day/ Date	Location	Road	Mile	Rating	Note
Wed. 7/21/04	Prairie du Chien	18	0	**	Came up on Tues., spent the night.
	Bridgeport	18	7	****	Crossed WI River and turned onto CR C. Nice twisting road along the river.
	Boscobel	133	30	****	Take 61 N and then turn on to CR S for a twisting good time.
	Blue River	133	48	****	Long way around to travel 8 miles but worth it.
	Dodgeville	18	78	***	Series of Co. roads over to here. Visited House on the Rock.
	Spring Green	23	96	***	Frank Lloyd Wright Center.
	Blue Mound	18 & 151	120	****	Roundabout route to the highest point in S. Wisconsin. Lots to see in this area.
	Sauk City	78	145	****	Another pretty stretch of 78.
	Baraboo	12	165	**	Visited Circus World. Beautiful antique circus wagons. Stopped for the night.
Thur. 7/22/04	Wisconsin Dells	12	15	*	Too commercial, got out fast.
	Richland	14	85	***	Took lots of back

	Location	Road	Mile	Rating	Note
	Center				roads and visited several parks.
	Gays Mills	171	113	****	To early for the apple harvest.
	Wauzeka	133	133	****	Followed the crooked Kickapoo River. Gave up on visiting Kickapoo Caverns. Road heavy gravel and straight up.
	Bridgeport	133	144	****	Decided to head home.
	Erie, IL	Moline Rd	280	****	Still love this drive.

Chapter 5: Prairie du Chien North

Day/ Date	Location	Road	Mile	Rating	Note
Tue. 8/10/04	Prairie du Chien, WI	35	0	*****	Starting from Prairie du Chien again. My birthday trip.
	Ferryville, WI	35	23	*****	Lovely ride along the river. The drive has been compared to the Rhine and Hudson River Valleys.
	Soldier's Grove	CR C	43	*****	20 miles of twisting skyline drive.
	Hillsboro	82	75	*****	All the roads are curvy and fun. Edge of Amish Country. Watch for horse-drawn vehicles.
	N of Westby	CR P	107	*****	County P is full of twists and hills. Keeps you on your toes.
	De Soto	35	139	*****	Calming down from the all the twists. Back along the river.

	LaCrosse	35	175	*****	Explored LaCrosse and surrounding area.
	Onalaska	35	177	*****	Made arrangement to use Lake Motel as base for further trips north.
	Onalaska	35	0	*****	Heading out again. Will go north and then start winding my way back home.
	Mindoro	CR D	16.5	*****	Learned about Spanferkel. Wonderful word, pig in German.
	West Salem	108	26	******	OMG putting in an extra star for this one. WOW Midwest's answer to Deal's Gap.
	Sparta	16	42	***	A welcome respite after 108. Saw world's largest bicycle.
	New Lisbon	80	79	****	Starting to head home. Still dizzy after 108.
	Erie, IL	Albany Rd	280	***	Fun trip.

Chapter 6: The North Country

Day/ Date	Location	Road	Mile	Rating	Note
Tue. 9/8/04	Onalaska, WI	35	0	****	Start of three-day trip. Hint of Fall.
	Trempealeau	35	18	****	Visited Trempealeau St. Park. Really pretty.
	Galesville	CR K to 54	26	***	Galesville has been claimed to be Garden of Eden. Okay.
	Black River Falls	54	73	****	Real pretty ride .
	"	12 & CR O	98	****	A nice circle ride

					through the state forest.
	Hatfield	E	109	****	Lake Arbutus, nice stop.
	Neillsville	95 & 73	128	*****	Highground veterans memorial, impressive.
	Osseo	10	161	****	Don't miss the Norske Nook, top rated restaurant, great food
	Arcadia	121	193	****	Nice drive, several interesting county roads.
	Fountain City	95	211	****	Skyline Drive, pretty but CRs more interesting.
	Galesville	93	271	****	Checked out numerous CRs.
	Onalaska	35	288	***	Lake motel looks good
Wed. 9/9/04	""	35	0	***	Starting another day.
	Arcadia	93	35	****	Checked out some more CRs.
	Cochran	35	59	****	Traveled by CR E & CR O, stunning road.
	Pepin	35	83	****	Lake Pepin, and nearby the birthplace of Laura Ingalls Wilder.
	Prescott	35	128	****	Several small river towns. Northern point in Wisconsin.
	State Line Park	10	129	****	Had a picnic lunch and watched the boats on the mouth of the St. Croix River.
	Ellsworth	10	147	****	Picked up some curd.
	Spring Valley	29	166	****	Visited the cave.
	Elmwood	72	173	***	UFO capital. Unsuccessful search for aliens.

	Downsville	72	184	****	Great food at the Creamery.
	Onalaska	35	290	****	Lots of winding around.
Thur. 9/10/04	Onalaska	35	0	****	Spending the day checking out more CRs before heading home.
	Tomah	16	90	****	40 miles as the crow flies but did a lot of CRs.
	Erie, IL	Moline Rd	300	****	Back home and ready for a rest.

Chapter 7: Marvelous Minnesota

Day/ Date	Location	Road	Mile	Rating	Note
Tue. 10/5/05	Onalaska, WI	35	0	****	Heading into MN. Leaves just beginning to turn. Late this year.
	Winona, MN	61	29	****	Four lane follows the river. Great view of the town from overlook..
	Kellogg	61	57	****	Lark Toy Company a must stop. Huge hand carved carousel. Large toy store.
	Wabasha	61	64	****	National Eagle Center. Nose to beak experience.
	Lake City	61	80	****	West shore of Lake Pepin, huge marina.
	Hastings	61	124	****	Back to the mouth of the St. Croix.
	Cannon Falls	19	141	***	Lunch at the Mill above the falls.
	Northfield	19	158	***	Town that brought

					down James/Younger gang.
	Zumbro Falls	60	193	***	Great drive over to Wabasha.
	Wabasha	61	230	****	Taking several CRs back to Onalaska.
	Onalaska	35	310	****	Another long day.
	""	35	0	***	More Minnesota.
Wed. 10/6/04	Rochester, MN	52	73	***	Just okay trip. Lots to see in Rochester
	Mantorville	57	91	***	Pretty town. The best food yet at Hubbell House.
	LaCrescent	61	176	****	Beautiful drives around LaCrescent.
	Onalaska	35	220	****	Local exploring, began to rain so went back and watched TV.
Thur. 10/17/04	Onalaska	35	0	***	Crisp fall day.
	Houston MN	16	25	****	Be sure to visit the Houston Nature Center
	Dexter	16	95	****	Beautiful ride,
	Austin	I90	111	**	Spam Museum,
	Harmony	52	169	***	Must do more exploring up here. Back in a couple of weeks.
	Erie, IL	Moline RD	360	****	Long Day.
Tue. 10/19/04	Lanesboro, MN	16	0	****	Pretty little town.
	Rt. 30	250N	20	****	Really nice ride both directions, hills & curves.
	Rt. 12	21S	27	****	Nice winding road
	Preston	16	35	****	Visit Mystery Cave.
	Caledonia	76	76	***	Lots of neat CRs in area.
	Brownsville	26	90	****	Lots of sweepers on CR 3.

	New Albin IA	26	108	****	Nice ride along the river.

Chapter 8: Iowa - More Than Just Cornfields

Day/ Date	Location	Road	Mile	Rating	Note
Tue. 10/19/04	Lansing, IA	26	120	****	Continuing on from Chapter 7.
	Marquette/ McGregor	CR X52	147	****	CR X52 is sandwiched between the river and bluffs.
	Erie, IL	Moline Rd	267	****	Getting back in familiar territory.
Mon. 10/25/04	Marquette/ McGregor	76	0	****	Picking up where we left off.
	Effigy Mounds National Monument	76	3	****	Get off the bikes and hike up the bluffs to a lookout point.
	Yellow River State Forest	CR B25	10	****	Beautiful ride through unspoiled area.
	Waukon	CR A52	30	****	Nice ride through the hills.
	Decorah	9	48	***	Interesting Nordic town.
	Spillville	52	57	***	Visit the clock museum, wonderful workmanship.
	Clermont	18	87	***	Still riding the hill country.
	McGregor	18	117	***	Finished the northern loop.
	Guttenberg	52	136	****	CR X56 is a great ride along the river. Stopped at Pike's Peak State Park.
	Balltown	CR CY9	158	****	Biker's favorite. Stop for lunch at Breitbach's for lunch. The oldest

					restaurant in Iowa.
	Sageville	3	169	****	A turn west here will take you around some twists on highway 3.
	Strawberry Point	3	219	***	Well it does have the world's largest strawberry
	Dubuque	20	272	****	Stopped for the night.

Chapter 9: Dubuque to the Quad Cities

Day/ Date	Location	Road	Mile	Rating	Note
Tue. 10/26/04	Dubuque	20	0	****	Visited the Aquarium and rode the cable car. Stunning view of the city & harbor.
	St. Donatus	52	13	****	Historic Luxembourg Village
	Bellevue	52	23	****	Beautiful River town. Fall colors breathtaking.
	Anamosa	64	78	***	Visited the National Motorcycle Museum.
	Sabula	64	140	***	Town located on an Island.
	Clinton	67	175	****	Bluffs and fall colors. Can't be beaten.
	Erie, IL	Albany Rd	195	***	Back home again.
Wed. 11/3/04	""	""	0	***	Heading to the Quad Cities by the scenic route.
	Clinton, IA	67	20	***	Stopped at the Arboretum. Fall colors again.
	LeClaire	67	60	***	Took side trips to visit Buffalo Bill Homestead,

					historical village. Buffalo Bill Museum.
	Davenport	67	70	***	Saw movie at IMAX theater.
	Erie, IL	Moline Rd	100	***	Must add in Cordova Rd. Nice ride home.

Appendix II

Towns, Sites, & Attractions

Find a destination here; refer to the Index for town and city page numbers in the book.

Albany, IL,
  Albany Mounds State
    Preserve
  Ammons Landing
  Julie's Café
  Mississippi Café
Alma, WI,
  Alma Marina
  Buena Vista Park
  Rieck's Lake Park
Alma Center, WI
  Strawberry Festival
Almont Tap
Anamosa, IA
  Anamosa Penitentiary
    Museum
  Grant Wood Art Gallery
  Grant Wood Memorial
    Park
  J&P Cycles
  National Motorcycle
Museum
  Pumpkinfest
Andrew, IA
  Andrew City Park
  Andrew Jackson
Demonstration Farm
  Andrew Jail Historical
    Site
Arcadia, WI,
  Arcadia Broiler & Dairy
    Days
  Carnegie Library
  Memorial Park, (Avenue
    of Heroes Walk)

Shanks Park
Pietrek Park,

Wisconsin Skyline
  Drive
Argyle, WI
  Toy Train Barn
Arkansas, WI
  Arkansas Creek Park
  (road to) Big Coulee
  Columbia Heights
  Plum Creek Valley
  Porcupine Valley
Austin, MN
  Hormel House
  Jay C. Hormel Nature
    Center
  Mower County
Historical Center
  Paramount Theater
  Rydjor Bike Museum
  Spam Museum
Avoca, WI
  Avoca Lakeside Park
  Avoca Prairie

Baldwin, IA
  Baldwin Marsh
  Eden Valley Nature
    Center
  Mill Rock Schoolhouse
  Tabor Home Vineyards
Balltown, IA
  Breitbach's
Bay City, WI
  Bay City Days

Conlin Cabin
River Bluffs Historical
Society
Waterfront Park
Bagley, WI
Jellystone Park
Barneveld, WI
Botham Vineyards and
Winery
Baraboo, WI
Circus World Museum
Bellevue, IA
Bellevue State Park
Garden Sanctuary for
Butterflies
Mont Rest
Potters Mill
Richman's Café
South Bluff Nature
Center
Belmont, WI
Belmont Mounds State
Park
First Territorial Capitol
Benton, WI
Benton Water Tower
Mazzuchelli Grave
St. Patrick's Catholic
Church
Swindler's Ridge
Museum
Village School House
Museum
Bettendorf, IA
Brenny's Motorcycle
Clinics
Black River Falls, WI
Karner Blue Butterfly
Festival
Pioneer Brewery
The Merchant General
Store
Wazee Lake,

Blair, WI
Cheese factory
Countryside Lefse
Factory
Blanchardville, WI
Blanchardville
Historical Society
Museum
Yellowstone Lake
Blue Mounds, WI
Blue Mounds State Park
Boaz, WI
Boaz Mastodon
Boscobel, WI
Boscobel Depot
Museum
Boscobel Hotel
Gideon Society
Brownsville, MN
Buffalo City, WI
Buffalo City Bash
Foelsch Riverside Park
Burr Oak, IA
Laura Ingalls Wilder
Park and Museum
Burr Oak Hotel

Caledonia, MN
Beaver Creek Valley
State Park
Camanche, IA
Blue Heron Eco Cruises
Camanche Days
Camanche Depot &
Museum
Cambells Island, IL
Riverside Park
Camp Douglas, WI
Camp Williams
Ice Age Nat'l Scientific
Reserve
Mill Bluff State Park
Volk Field

Wisconsin National
Guard Memorial
Library and Museum
Cannon Falls, MN
Cannon Falls Arts
Festival
Cannon Cruising Days
Car Show
Minnieska Park
Stone Mill
Vasa Museum
Canton, MN
Cashton, WI
Amish tour
St. Mary's Church
St. Mary's Ridge
Cassville, W
Car Ferr
Nelson Dewey State Park
Stonefield Village
Castle Rock State Park, IL
Cataract, WI
Cataract Sportsmen Club
Little Falls RR & Doll
Museum
Monroe County Local
History Room
Museum and
Library
Wegner Grotto
Chaseburg, WI
Heartland Tradesman's
Museum
Cheyenne Valley, WI
Cheyenne Valley
Heritage Society
Churchtown, IA
Cheese store
Clermont, IA
Clermont Opera House
Henderson Statue
Larrabee Bank
Larrabee School Lincoln

Statue
Montauk
Riegel Blacksmith Shop
Clinton, IA
Art in the Park
Balloons in June
Bickellhaupt Arboretum
Clinton Area Showboat,
Clinton Harley
Davidson
Clinton Lumber Kings
Clinton Symphony
Orchestra
Eagle Point Park
Gateway Contemporary
Ballet
Historical Society
Museum
Mississippi Belle II
River Arts Center
Riverview Park
Soaring Eagle Nature
Center
Riverboat Days
Cobb, WI
Blackhawk Lake
Recreation Area
Corn boil
Cochran, WI
Cochran-Buffalo City 4th
of July
Coon Valley, WI
Norskeldalen Nature
and Heritage
Center
Skumsrud Heritage
Farm
Cordova, IL
Cordova Dragstrip
Scenic Road Restaurant
Cresco, IA
Heritage Train
Iowa Wrestling Hall of

227

Fame
Kellow House
Welcome Center,
Cuba City, WI
Café on the Main
Carr Cheese Factory
Gile Cheese Store
Street of the Presidents
Weber's Processing
Plant
Splinter Park
Water tower, 66

Dakota, MN
Apple Blossom Drive
Darlington, WI
Lafayette County
Historical Society
and Depot Museum
Davenport, IA
Adler Theater
Bix Beiderbecke
Memorial Jazz
Festival
Hawkeye Motor Works
Putnam Museum &
IMAX Theater
River Center
Sturgis on the River
Wiebler's Harley
Davidson
Decorah, IA
Luther College
Porter House Museum
Vesterheim Norwegian
American Museum
Willowglen Nursery
Deer Grove, IL
Arnie's Happy Spot
Sandy Pine Elk Farm
Dexter. MN,
Truck Stop
Diamond Bluff, WI

Sea Wing
The Gem
Dickeyville, WI
Grotto
Dixon, IL
Arch
Lincoln Memorial
Reagan Boyhood Home
Reagan Trail
Dodgeville, WI
Courthouse Inn
Folklore Village
Governor Dodge State
Park
Iowa County
Courthouse,
Iowa County Historical
Society Cabin
Land's End Outlet Store
Dorchester, IA
Downsville, WI
The Creamery
Restaurant & Inn
Dubuque, IA
Diamond Jo Riverboat
Casino
Dubuque Arboretum &
Botanical Gardens
Dubuque County
Fairgrounds
Dubuque Greyhound
Park & Casino
Dubuque Museum of the
Arts
Dubuque Symphony
Orchestra
Eagle Point Park
Fenelon Place Elevator
Five Flags Civic Center
Grand Opera House,
Grant Wood Collection
Julian Dubuque
Monument

Lock & Dam
Marshall Park
McAleece Park &
  Recreation
  Complex
Mines of Spain
  Recreation Area
Miss Dubuque
  Riverboat
National Mississippi
  River Museum
  and Aquarium
Port of Dubuque
Spirit of Dubuque
  Riverboat
Wilwert's Harley
  Davidson/Buell
Dyersville, IA
  Basilica of St. Francis
    Xavier
  Becker Woodcarving
    Museum
  Dyer-Botsford Doll
    Museum
  Field of Dreams Movie
    Site
  National Farm Toy
    Museum
  Plaza Antique Mall
East Bennett Lutheran
Church, WI
East Dubuque, IL
  Gramercy Park
  Hopewell Indian
    Mound
Eau Galle, WI
  Lakeside Wedding
    Chapel
Elizabeth, IL
  Apple River Ft. State
    Historic Site
  Bishop's Busy Big Store
  Chicago Great Western

Railway Depot
  Museum
Eshelman Pottery
Georgetown Bridge
Terrapin Ridge
Edgewood, IA
  Bixby State Preserve
  Clayton County,
    Delaware County
    Rodeo Days
Eleva, WI
  Adams Creek
  Beef River Valley
  Big Creek
  Buffalo River
  Eleva Broiler Days
  Eleva Pond
  Eleva Ridge
Elkader, IA
  Big Springs Trout
    Hatchery
  Carter House Museum
  City Park
  Elkader Opera House
  Keystone Bridge
  Motor Mill Historic Site
  Osborne Visitor Nature
    and Welcome Center
  Turkey River
Ellsworth, WI,
  Beldenville Old Car
    Club Show
  Cheese Curd Days
  Pierce County Fair
  Polka Fest
Elmwood, WI
  UFO Days
Erie, IL
  Depot
  Glass Rail
  Other Place
  Pink Pony
  PJ's

Russ' Café
The Greens
Ettrick, WI
   Beaver Creek
   Ettrick Fun Days

Farley, IA
   Farley Speedway
Fennimore, WI
   Fennimore Doll and Toy
     Museum
   Fennimore Railroad
     Museum
   Oakwood Nature Park
Fenton, IL
   Payne's Grocery
Ferryville, WI
Festina, IA
   World's Smallest Church
Fort Atkinson, IA
   Fort Atkinson State
     Preserve and
     Museum
   Rendezvous
Fort McCoy, WI
   Driving tour
   Pine View Recreation
     Area
   Whitetail Ridge
     Recreation Area
Fountain City, WI
   Elmer's Auto & Toy
     Museum,
   Fountain City Festival
   Hilltop Ballroom
   Historical Society
     Museum
   Historical Water
     Fountain
   Merrick State Park,
   Old Time Farm Fest
   Polka Fest
   Prairie Moon Museum

     and Sculptured
     Gardens
   Rock in the House
   Scenic Overlook Deck
Froelich Historical Village, IA
Fulton, IL
   Artistry in Glass
   Bear Land Trading
     Post
   Calico Creations
   Dutch Days
     Celebration
   Freedom Motor Sports
   Fulton Fiber Mill
   Great River Antiques
   Heritage Canyon
   Lock and Dam
   Martin House Museum
   Paddlewheel Pizza
   Shell Station
   Windmill

Galena, IL
   Belvedere House and
     Gardens
   Dowling House
   Grant Home
   Galena Trolley Co.
   Jo Daviess County
     Historical Society &
     Museum
   Old Market House
   Peace In the Union
   Wilwert's Harley
     Davidson
Galesville, WI
   Apple Affair
   Arnold House
   Artic Springs
   Brush Trophy Room
     Museum
   Cance House
   Clark House B&B

Gale College Historic
Site
Highcliff Park
Lake Marinuka
McGilvray Bottoms
Goodview, MN
Goodview Days
Grand Detour, IL
John Deere home,
Colonial Rose B&B
Gratiot, WI
Truck Stop
Great River Bluffs State Park,
MN
Gulf of Mexico
Guttenberg, IA
German Fest
Lockmaster's House
Museum
Mississippi River
Aquarium

Hager City, WI
Bow & Arrow
Hampton, IL
Black's Store
Heritage Center
Hanover, IL
Apple River Falls
Chestnut Mountain
Goldmoor Inn
Harmony, MN
Harmony Toy Museum
Niagara Cave
Harper's Ferry, IA
Rest Area
Scenic Ridgeview
Exotic Animal Ranch
Hastings, MN
Afton State Park
Courthouse
Lake Rebecca
Rivertown Days

Schaar's Bluff Picnic
Area
Spring Lake Park
Vermillion River Falls
Hatfield, WI
Lake Arbutus
Hegg, WI
Highland, WI
Highland Village Park
Spurgeon Vineyards &
Winery
Hillsboro, WI
Cesky Den
Hillsboro Museum &
Log Cabin
Hixton, WI
Cain's Orchard
Hokah, MN
Como Falls
Mount Tom
Holmen, WI
Deer Wood Park
Kornfest
Houston, MN
Alice the Owl
Cody the Buffalo
Cody Mercantile
Houston Nature Center
Hustler, WI
Petroglyphs
Twin Bluffs
Hyde, WI
Hyde Mill
Illiniwek County Forest
Preserve, IL
Independence, WI
City Hall & Opera
House
Independence Days
St. Peter & Paul
Catholic Church

Kellogg, MN

Lark Toy Company
Mini-golf
Moose Tracks Museum
Prairie Sand Dunes
Watermelon Fest
Kent, IL
    Blackhawk War
       Memorial
Kickapoo River, WI

LaCrescent, MN
    Apple Blossom Drive
LaCrosse, WI
    City Brewery Tour
    Granddad's Bluff
    Hixon House
    Island Girl
    Julia Belle Swain
    LaCrosse Queen
    Riverside Museum
    Swarthout Museum
LaFarge, WI
    Kickapoo Reserve
Lake City, MN
    Hok-Si-La Park
    Marina
    Water Ski Days
Lancaster, WI
    Cunningham Museum
    Grant County
       Courthouse
    Grant River
    Klondike Park
    Memorial Park
    Pleasant Ridge
       Cemetery
    Ryland Park
Lanesboro, MN
    Art In the Park
    Buffalo Bill Days
    Commonweal Theater
    Inspiration Point
    Lanesboro Fish

       Hatchery
    Lanesboro Historical
       Museum
    Oktoberfest
    Sykkle Tour
    Sylvan Park
Lansing, MN
    Commercial Fishing
       Museum
    Mt. Hosmer
LeClaire, IA
    Buffalo Bill Museum
    Mississippi River Tug
       Fest
    Sneaky Pete's
Leland, WI
    Natural Bridge State
       Park
Lena, IL
    Lake Le-Aqua-Na State
       Park
    Kolb-Lena Cheese Co
    Torkelson Cheese
       Factory
    watertower
LeRoy, MN
    Carnegie Library
    Lake Louise State Park
    Prairie School Bank
Long Grove, IA
    Alexander Brownlie
       Sod Home
    Dan Nagle's Walnut
       Grove Pioneer
       Village
    Scott County Park
Luana, IA
Lynxville, WI
    Cigar Store Indian
    Lock & Dam 9

Maiden Rock, WI
    Flood Run

Summerfest
Mantorville, MN
    Chocolate Shoppe
    City Park
    Hubble House
        Restaurant
Maquoketa, IA
    Costello's Old Mill
        Gallery
    Huntsville Interpretive
        Center
    Huntsville Lime Kilns
    Jackson County
        Historical Society
        Museum
    Kleppe's Motor Sports
    Maquoketa Caves State
        Park
    Old City Hall Gallery
Mather, WI
    Central Wisconsin
        Conservation
        Area
McGregor/Marquette, IA
    Effigy Mounds
    Isle of Capri,
    McGregor Historical
        Museum
    Marquette Depot
        Museum
    Pike's Peak State Park
    Spook Cave
Meadow Valley, WI
    Meadow Valley
        Ranger Station
Melrose, WI
    Parks
Merrillon, WI
    Double T Quik Stop &
        Barbershop
    Halls Creek
    Oakwood Lake
    Trow Lake

Millville, IA
    Car Ferry to Cassville,
        WI
Mindoro, WI
    Spanferkel
        Celebration
Mineral Point, WI
    American Players
        Theatre
    Gundry House
    Mineral Point
        Railway Museum
    Pendarvis House
    Shake Rag Alley
Modena, WI
    Old Mill & Waterfall
Moline, IL
    Mark of the Quad
        Cities
    Fun Mart Cycle Center
Monroe, WI
    Cheese Days
    Green County
        Courthouse
    Historic Cheese
        Making Center
    Joseph Huber Brewery
    Limburger Cheese
    Monroe Depot
    Swiss cheese
    Swiss Colony
Mondovi, WI
    Arboretum
    Buffalo Store &
        Gallery
    Friendship Days
    Mirror Lake
    Veterans Memorial
Monmouth, IA
    Four-D-Acres
    Frantzen Family Used
        Tractors & Parts
    Gib Marcucci Stables,

Montfort, WI
Windfarm
Monticello, IA
Bowstring Bridge
Pictured Rocks Park
Riverside Gardens
Stone Bridge
Mt. Carroll, IL
Campbell Learning
Center, (Shimer
College)
Civil War Monument
Timber Lake Resort
and Campground
Timber Lake
Playhouse
Willow Folk Festival
Willow Inn B&B
Mt. Horeb, WI
Cave of the Mounds
Little Norway
Mustard Museum
Stewart Park
Mt. Ida, WI
Mt. Sterling, WI
Mt. Sterling Cheese
Co-op
Morrison, IL,
Morrison Rockwood
State Park
Covered Bridge
Hill & Dale B&B
Muscoda, WI
Morel Mushroom
Festival

Nacedah, WI
Nacedah Nat'l
Wildlife Refuge
Neilsville, WI
Chatty Belle
Highground Benefit
Motorcycle

Rally
Highground Veterans
Memorial
Nelson, WI
Hang gliding
Nelson Cheese Factory
Tiffany Wildlife Area
New Albin, IA
Fish Farm Mounds
New Glarus, WI
Historical Swiss Village
New Glarus Brewery
New Glarus Woods
State Park
Primrose Winery
Wilhelm Tell Festival
New Lisbon, WI
Indian Mounds Park
New Lisbon Memorial
Library
New Vienna, IA
Heritage House
Museum
Nerstrand Big Woods
State Park
Dwarf trout lily
Nora, IL
Northfield, MN
Carleton College
Defeat of Jesse James
Days
Northfield Historical
Society
St. Olaf College

Onalaska, WI
LaCrosse Area Harley
Davidson
Lake Motel
Lake Onalaska
Black River
Omni-Center
Thunder Ride

Two Brothers Honda
Steiger Power Sports
Van Riper Park
Ontario, WI
  Kinney Valley Alpacas
  Wildcat Mt. State Park
Oregon, IL
  Autumn on Parade
  Lowden Park
  Maxson Riverside
    Restaurant
  Pride of Oregon
  Stronghold
Osseo, WI
  Lake Martha Days
Celebration
  Norske Nook
    Restaurant & Bakery
  Stoddard Park

Pepin, WI
  Great River Birding
    Festival
  Lake Pepin Players
  Laura Ingalls Wilder
    Days
  Laura Ingalls Wilder
    Museum
  Little House Wayside
  Pepin Depot Museum
Peterson, MN
  Lillian's House of the
    Seven Gables
Pickwick, MN
  Mill Day
  Pickwick Mill
Pigeon Falls, WI
  Buena Vista Wayside
    Park
  Ekern Park
  Pigeon Creek
    Evangelical
    Lutheran Church

Pigeon Falls Lions Club
Plain, WI
  Cedar Grove Cheese
  Lourdes Grotto
  St. Anne's Shrine
  St. Luke's Catholic
    Church
Platteville, WI
  Mining Museum
  Rollo Jamison Museum
  Roundtree Gallery
  Univ. of Wisconsin
    Platteville
  World's Biggest M
Polo, IL
  Aplington House
    Museum
  Burns House
  Henry School
  Town & Country Days
    Festival
  White Pines State Park
Port Byron, IL
  Great River Tug Fest
Postville, IA
  Diversity Garden
  Postville Visitors Center
Potosi-Tennyson, WI
  Badger Huts
  Catfish Festival
  Grant River Recreation
    Campground
  Hickory Hill City Park
  Passage through Time
    Museum
  St. John Mine
  The Point
Prairie du Chien, WI
  Crawford County
    Courthouse
  Ft. Crawford Museum
  Prairie Villa
    Rendezvous

St. Gabriel's Catholic
Church
Territorial Prison
Villa Louis
Prescott, WI
Kinickinnic State Park
Preston, MN
Forestville
Jailhouse Inn
Mystery Cave
Princeton, IA
Bridge's Waterfront
Cody Homestead
Kernan's Riverview
Restaurant
Prophetstown, IL
Eclipse Square
Prophetstown Historical
Museum
Prophetstown State Park

Rapids City, IL
Brother's Family
Restaurant
Park
Read's Landing MN
Overlook
Readstown, WI,
Civil War Cemetery
Riverside Park
Red Wing, MN
Anderson Center for
Interdisciplinary
Studies
Frontenac State Park
Goodhue County
Museum
Great Minnesota Morel
Festival
Red Wing Arts Assn.
Gallery
Red Wing Depot
Red Wing Shoes

Sheldon Performing
Arts Theater
Sorin Bluff
Richland Center, WI
Center Color Fiesta
Krouskop Park
Mayan Temple
Red Door Gallery
Ridgeway, IA
Beadle Park
Ridgeway, WI
Ghost
River Falls, WI
Hoffman Park
Kansas City Chiefs
Training Camp
Kinnickinnic River
Mound Park
Old Falls Theater
Rochester, MN
Heritage House
Mayo Clinic
Mayowood
Mayo Civic Center
Plummer Mansion
Rock Falls, IL
Workman's Harley
Davidson
Rock Island, IL
Blackhawk State Park
Hobart's Cycle
The District
Tri City Motor Sales
Rollingstone, MN
Luxembourg Heritage
Museum
Rushford, MN
Depot visitors' center
Root River

Sabula, IA
Jackson Co. Welcome
Center

South Sabula Lakes
Park
Sageville, IA
St. Donatus, IA
Gehlen House
Kalmes Restaurant
Kalmes General Store
Luxembourg Days
Pieta Chapel
St. Donatus Catholic
Church
St. John's German
Lutheran Church
Way of the Cross
Sauk City/ Prairie du
Sac Cow Chip
Nationals
Savanna, IL
Cherokee Junction
Harvest Moon
Emporium
Iron Horse Social Club
Looney Linda's
Mississippi Palisades
State Park
Poopy's Motorcycle
Parts & Accessories
Poopy's Pub
Pulford Opera House
Antique Mall
Savanna/Subula Bridge
Scales Mound, IL
Charles Mound
Country House Grocery
Countryside Feeds
Scales Mound
Scotch Grove, IA
Edinburgh Ghost Town
and Museum
Shullsburg WI
Badger Mine &
Museum
Badger Park

Brewster Café &
Cheese Store
Gravity Hill
Silvis, IL
Brenny's Cycle Works
Soldier's Grove, WI
Solar City
Sparta, WI
Butterfest
Deke Slayton Memorial
Space & Bike
Museum
Monroe County
Museum
World's Largest Bicycle
Spillville, IA
Bily Clock Museum
Bouska Schoolhouse
Log Cabin
Inwood Pavilion
Polka Fest
Riverside Park
St. Wenceslaus Church
Soldiers and Sailors
Museum
Spring Green, WI
American Player's
Theatre
House on the Rock
Peck's Fruit Market
Taliesin
Tower Hill State Park
Spring Grove, MN
Ballard House Museum
Christmas Village
Wood Spinner Shop
Spring Valley, MN
Wilder Museum
Spring Valley, WI
Crystal Cave
Eau Galle Recreation
Area
Spring Valley Dam

Days

Sterling, IL
    Dillon Home
    Sinnissippi Park
Stockholm, WI
    Stockholm Art Festival
Stockton, IL
    Stockton Historical
        Museum
Stockton, MN
    George Hinton
        Memorial Park
Stone City, IA
    Grant Wood Art
        Festival
Stoddard, WI
Strawberry Point, IA
    Backbone State Park
    Wilder Historical
        Museum
    World's Largest
        Strawberry
Strum, WI
    Crystal Lake
    Crystal Lake
        Campground
Tampico, IL
    Birthplace of Ronald
        Reagan
    Dutch Diner
Thomson, IL
    McGinnis Market
    Railroad Museum
    Thomson Causeway
    Watermelon Days
Tomah, WI
    Cranberry Festival
    Cranberry Museum
    Gillett Park
    Tomah Area Historical
        Society Museum
    Wisconsin Dairyland
    National Tractor/Truck

Pull

Upper Great Lakes

Viroqua, WI
    Historic Temple
        Theater
    Wild West Days
Viola, WI
    Horse & Colt Show

Wabasha, MN
    Grumpy Old Men
    National Eagle Center
    Slippery's Bar & Grill
Warren, IL
    Warren Community
        Building
Warrens, WI
    Cranberry Festival
    Wetherby's Cranberry
        Marsh
    McMullen Memorial
        County Park
    Wisconsin Cranberry
        Discovery Center
Waukon, IA
    Allamakee Historical
        Center & Museum
    Sweeney's House of
        Clocks
    Waukon Power Sports
Wazeka, WI
    Kickapoo Caverns
    Lower Wisconsin
        River Genealogical
        and Historical
        Research Center
Westby, WI
    Coon Prairie Church
    Syttende Mai
    Thorsen House
        Museum

Three Chimney's Rock
Westby Cooperative
    Creamery
Westby House Inn
West Salem, WI
    Dairy Days
    Hamlin Garland Home
    Palmer/Gullickson
        Home
    Thomas Leonard Home
Whitehall, WI
    Beef & Dairy Days
    Farmer's Market
Wilton, WI
    Wilton Lions Club
    Wilton Village Park
    Wilton Wood Turtle
        Days
Winona, MN
    Big Muddy River
        Rendezvous
    Garvin Heights
    Julius C. Wilkie
Steamboat Center
    Lake Park
    Levee Park
    Merchant's Bank
    Polish Apple Days
    Polish Cultural
        Institute
    Polish Heritage Days
    Steamboat Days
    Victorian Days

Watkins Heritage
    Museum,
Windom Park
Winona County
    Historical Society
    Armory Museum
Winona National Bank
    World's Fair
Winslow, IL
    Paradise Cove Park
    River Days
        Celebration
Wisconsin Dells
    Ducks
    Lost Canyon
    Lower Dells
    Upper Dells
Wyalusing, WI
    Wyalusing State Park
Wyoming IA
    Wyoming Historical
        Museum

Yellow River State Forest
    Little Paint Creek
    Paint Creek

Zumbroto, MN
    Carnegie Library
    Covered Bridge Park
    State Theater

Index of Towns & Cities

Index of People

ABOUT THE AUTHOR

Kay Fellows lives in Erie, Illinois. She has lived her entire life in Northwestern Illinois at the southern edge of the Upper Mississippi Valley and has traveled extensively in the area by car, RV, and motorcycle.

Her interests include motorcycles, horses, light aircraft, writing, and photography.

She has worked for the *Whiteside News Sentinel* and *The Review* for several years writing feature articles, and her work has also appeared in several magazines including *Kitplanes, Aero Sport Connection, Young Rider, Western Horse, Reminisce Extra, Rural Heritage,* and *Equus.*

Printed in the United States
64099LVS00004B/25-30

9 781892 216564